Anthony Masters won the John Llewellyn Rhys Memorial Prize with his novel, *The sea horse*, and was runner-up for the same prize with a collection of short stories, *A pocketful of rye*. In the '70s he wrote several thrillers for Constable under the pseudonym of Richard Tate. In collaboration with Falklands hero, Captain Nick Barker, Masters has written two novels – *Red ice* and *Rig* – and his books for children include *Dream palace, Shell shock, Dead man at the door* and *Raven*. His two crime novels, *Murder is a long time coming* and *Confessional*, were published in 1991 and 1993 respectively.

He has also published a biography of Nancy Astor, one of Charles Henry Maxwell Knight (*The man who was M*) and *Literary agents*, a collection of biographical studies of prominent writers who were also involved in work for the secret services.

He lives with his wife and children near Heathfield in Sussex.

Philip Falle has been a journalist with the *Jersey Evening Post* since 1973. Prior to that he served in the States of Jersey Police for almost a decade.

He began working on the story of Nicholas and Elizabeth Newall within a few days of their disappearance in October 1987 and, like his former colleagues in the Jersey police, soon became convinced that Roderick and Mark Newall knew more than they had told detectives.

He lives in Jersey with his wife Marion, who is also a journalist, and has three daughters, a son who is now following his father's footsteps in the police service, and two grandchildren.

Also by Anthony Masters

FICTION

A pocketful of rye (1964)
The sea horse (1966)
A literary lion (1968)
Conquering heroes (1969)
The donor (1970)
The syndicate (1971)
The dead travel fast (1971)
The emperor on ice (1973)
Birds of a bloodied feather
(1974)
Red ice (with Nicholas
Barker, 1986)
Rig (with Nicholas Barker,
1990)
Murder is a long time coming
(1991)
Confessional (1993)

NON-FICTION

The summer that bled (1972)
Bakunin (1974)
Bedlam (1977)
Rosa Lewis (1977)
Inside marbled halls (1979)
Nancy Astor (1981)
The man who was M (1984)
Literary agents (1987)

CHILDREN'S FICTION

Badger (1986)
Streetwise (1987)
Dream palace (1988)
Frog (1989)
Mel's run (1989)
Nobody's child (1989)
All the fun of the fair (1989)
Cat burglars (1989)
Siege (1990)
African queen (1990)
Shell shock (1990)
Nightmare in New York (1990)
Battle for the badgers (1990)
Sad song of the whale (1990)
Dolphin's revenge (1990)
Monsters on the beach (1990)
The song of the dead (1990)
The seventh stream (1990)
Travellers' tales (1990)
Playing with fire (1990)
Spirit of the condor (1991)
Gorilla mountain (1991)
Vanishing point (1991)
Klondyker (1991)
Traffic (1991)
Crab (1992)
Tunnel terror (1992)
The transformation of
Jennifer Howard (1992)
Scary tales to tell in the dark
(1992)
Dead man at the door (1992)

The

NEWALL MURDERS

◆

Anthony Masters & Philip Falle

Constable · London

First published in Great Britain 1994 by Constable and Company Ltd
3 The Lanchesters, 162 Fulham Palace Road, London W6 9ER
Copyright © 1994 by Anthony Masters and Philip Falle
The right of Anthony Masters and Philip Falle to be
identified as the authors of this work has been asserted
by them in accordance with the Copyright, Designs
and Patents Act 1988
ISBN 0 09 473520 4
Set in Linotron Sabon 11 pt by Rowland Phototypesetting Ltd
Printed in Great Britain by St Edmundsbury Press Ltd
both of Bury St Edmunds, Suffolk

A CIP catalogue record for this book
is available from the British Library

'If you hang on to the past – you'll die a little every day.'
Cape Fear

All photographs were taken by Gary Grimshaw, except the following:

Mark Newall (5) by Mail Newspapers plc

Crow's Nest (10) and Roderick directs the police . . . (16) by Brian Smith

The Sea Crest Hotel (13) by Neil Munns (The Press Association)

ILLUSTRATIONS

Between pages 64 and 65

1 Nicholas Newall
2 Elizabeth Newall
3 Roderick Newall at St Michael's School, Jersey
4 Mark Newall at the same school
5 Mark Newall, January 1991
6 Roderick Newall in St Helier, Jersey, April/May
   1988
7 Mark Newall with his father's twin, Stephen, and
   Aunt Gaye
8 Roderick (right) and Mark after Kenneth Newall's
   funeral, 1988
9 Maureen and David Ellam
10 Crow's Nest, Greve de Lecq, Jersey
11 The Newalls' bungalow at Clos de l'Atlantique, St
    Brelade, Jersey
12 The bedroom and sitting room of the Newalls'
    home
13 The Sea Crest Hotel and Restaurant
14 Detective Inspector Martin Fitzgerald with axe and
    rice flail

15 The search at the scene of the fire at Greve de Lecq
16 Roderick directs the police to where his parents' bodies were buried, November, 1993

PROLOGUE

After he had murdered his parents Roderick Newall would park his car near their unmarked graves in the field near the beach of Greve de Lecq in Jersey. However dangerously revealing his presence was, he must have been drawn to watch over them. The ferocity of the murders had never left him, despite the fact that he could only remember glimpses rather than sequences. He must have felt closer to them now they were silent, buried in the same grave, the seasons maturing the earth above them; yet the images of what he had done besieged him – the blows, the blood, the horror of it all, the panicky cleaning up after the carnage.

As Roderick drove away he would no doubt try and associate himself personally with the murders, finding the concept still incredible yet remembering all too clearly his parents' obsession with each other and the fact that they had seemed to have little need for him and his younger brother Mark. Nicholas and Elizabeth Newall were sufficient for each other.

Driving past the bay with the surf rolling up the sand, Roderick may have imagined he heard the school bell his father would ring to summon his sons back to the house when they were children. He and Mark were appendages – not offspring – and the strident bell was reminiscent of the days at the boarding school where they had been sent at the tender age of seven. As a result the Newall brothers had formed their own bond of necessity, knowing they would never be invited inside the sacred intimacy of their parents' love for each other – a love that seemed policed by their authoritarian, dominating father. They were always condemned to be outsiders.

1

Nicholas Park Newall was murdered standing by the fireplace in his home at 9 Clos de l'Atlantique. He was repeatedly battered around the head and his blood sprayed in a great arc, hitting both the ceiling and the wall. This barbaric attack followed a family dinner at a nearby restaurant on 10th October 1987, to celebrate his wife Elizabeth's forty-eighth birthday. She was killed in the same way in the bedroom, and the assault was again so ferocious that her blood also shot to considerable heights.

David and Maureen Ellam, who had bought the Newalls' former home, the Crow's Nest, and were amongst their most intimate friends, vividly remembered a visit they received from them earlier on 10th October. 'There was something distressing them both,' Maureen recalled. 'They hadn't fallen out, but something was upsetting them. Elizabeth said that they would be spending more and more time on the island.'

This was a strange, inexplicable comment, and as Nicholas and Elizabeth were both to die in the early hours of the following morning, their mood and this statement were crucial. Certainly the Newalls could not have been curtailing their activities through lack of money, for Nicholas's Uncle Kenneth, who lived in Sark, had made a joint pre-decease bequest to Nicholas and his twin brother, Stephen, who lived in Scotland. The sum was in the region of half a million pounds. Even before Kenneth's gift the Newalls had been moderately well off, and Nicholas was a Lloyds name. Although every penny, largely derived from investments, was counted, they still managed to own a yacht and an additional house in Spain, so it struck Maureen as extremely odd when Elizabeth confided that 'they would be spending more time on the island', particularly as the Newalls normally lived in Spain for considerable periods each year.

Nicholas had always been more than careful about the management of their money. Maureen Ellam remembered that Nicholas did not like to see any money wasted. He was even critical of his wife's handling of their financial affairs, telling Maureen that Elizabeth had lost quite a bit on investments. Excluding her from their discussions, he would often ask Maureen privately what she would do.

Elizabeth, however, had always been interested in the stock market and enjoyed following the fortunes of her stocks and shares. The Newalls were both highly competitive and appreciated the skill and challenge required. Losses, though, were something that Nicholas could not permit and eventually he handed over the management of his investments to his younger son, Mark, who was a fund manager in a finance house on the island. Maureen Ellam remembered that, 'In December 1986, Mark told me several times he was handling all the money. I was pleased, because that was better than Elizabeth doing it. I had confidence in his ability.'

Mark must have been successful: during the considerable periods his parents spent in Spain, he ran their affairs and had power of attorney over their assets and bank account. For several years, his father, who had been a member of the Outhwaite Syndicate, had like so many other Lloyds names been paying back approximately £30,000 a year and had, in 1986, sold the family home for £240,000, buying a small bungalow for £85,000. Using his considerable financial verve, Mark, however, was rapidly able to make good Nicholas's deficit. As a result he was taking an agreed 30% from the profits while Roderick had 10%.

Nicholas and Elizabeth Newall came from wealthy families and had met at New Park School, St Andrews, where they had both been teachers. They had married in Scotland on 20th December 1963. Nicholas's private income came from family interests in the Strathclyde shipbuilding industry. They had two children. Roderick Innes Nelson Newall was born on 11th April 1965 in Glasgow and Mark Stephen Nelson Newall was born 22nd June 1966 at St Andrews. In the late 1960s Nicholas and Elizabeth abandoned their professions as schoolteachers, bought a yacht and planned to set sail for the West Indies. Sailing had become a major interest in their lives and both were experienced enough to handle their boat and to care for their two small boys at the same time. They had invested their money and knew that if they lived modestly it should be possible to survive without having to work for a living. To undertake such a scheme needed considerable drive and a form of tunnel vision – both of which Nicholas possessed in quantity. Providing he was sufficiently immersed in the task at hand, he was happy; what he resented was the trivial structure of everyday life. He often came across as pompous, arrogant and dominating, sure of his sailing prowess but totally uninterested in domestic practicalities, where he was lazy, incompetent and withdrawn. 'If he didn't want to know you, you'd think, what a pig of a man. That was my first impression of him,' Maureen admitted. Her husband David agreed. 'That was his voice, he'd cut you off, cut you out. Once you had got through that voice, then you were there.' Even so, once roused, Nicholas Newall's anger was 'silent and complete. Bottled and silent and he would be all white,' Maureen reflected, adding that Elizabeth was very much the opposite. A physical education instructor, she loved sport and was a compulsive telephone caller. Like Nicholas, however, she had little interest in domestic matters. Maureen, who had grown close to her, said that there were very few people she felt quite so easy with. 'She was very quick-witted, quick-thinking. I soothed her, that was my role in life.' Maureen Ellam went on to state that Elizabeth Newall was 'in a permanent state of being up the wall – she was like a big child. The trouble was, when there were slight problems with the boys, I really thought she was getting it all out of proportion again. That's how she was. She was completely single-minded . . . Nicholas and I would look at her with a grin, you know, she was like our child. He [Nicholas] had a soulmate in me. For the first time, I felt, he had somebody who stood back and was amused by her, by her naughtiness sometimes, exactly as he was himself.'

Maureen also said, 'I loved his wife in exactly the same way as he [Nicholas] loved her. It was almost as if he believed that nobody else but him understood Elizabeth like I did.'

Perhaps it was partly due to the inherited money, but even to those who knew them well the Newalls appeared to be almost larger than life, pushing everything to its limits. 'They drove their cars hard, loved wine and spirits and were able to hold them. We never saw them out of control through drink,' said a couple who had been their friends for many years.

En route to the West Indies, the Newalls made a stop-over at Jersey to pick up a nanny for the boys, but shortly after they had put to sea again, the unfortunate nanny was taken ill and they were forced to return to the island. As a result, Nicholas and Elizabeth explored Jersey – and fell in love with it. The rocky and dramatic coastline, the distinctive identity with its own parliament and legal system, the welcome tax laws – all these appealed to Nicholas's sense of freedom and individuality. He decided they would go no further for he felt that Jersey was his kind of place.

Initially, they bought a house called Martello Lodge at St Brelade's Bay but in 1972 the family moved from there to the Crow's Nest, a property that overlooked the spectacularly beautiful bay called Greve de Lecq.

Later on, in 1977, Nicholas and Elizabeth bought a small villa at Javea in the south of Spain and spent many months there, sailing in the sun. Neither were exactly lotus eaters, but they both took such a genuine pleasure in each other's company that they were loath to have it interrupted – even by the children.

Jersey, however, never lost its appeal for them, Nicholas finding the tax laws particularly attractive. The island is of course an international finance centre, better known as a tax haven, and one of its main industries is money. It is not part of the UK and has a separate parliament which sets its own level of taxation for income. As Jersey is not part of the European Community, and with income tax at a maximum of 20 per cent, the island is attractive to banks, other financial institutions and foreign investors.

When they first arrived on the island, Nicholas Newall

taught at a couple of prep schools, for he felt he needed to supplement his income as well as have an occupation. He enjoyed teaching and his second post was at St Michael's Prep School which Roderick and Mark attended as pupils. The teaching also appealed to his dominating, narrow nature; children should be taught and they should obey. Elizabeth, meanwhile, whose nature was so much more frivolous, undertook a little supply teaching and strenuously played tennis. Even here, however, Elizabeth's competitive spirit prevailed: she took all sport extremely seriously and even when playing against close friends was always determined to win.

Later, Nicholas was diagnosed as having the viral infection ME, which led to him giving up teaching at fifty-two and taking to his bed for days at a time. The infection can be linked with bursts of depression and he was continually worried about money, going to the most extraordinary, panic-based economies, such as acquiring a motor-scooter to collect his newspapers from the local newsagents, having decided that his car's petrol consumption was too expensive for such a small trip. It was a strange economy from a man with two houses and a yacht – however modest. What is more, to qualify as a Lloyds name, Nicholas Newall must have possessed at least £250,000 in disposable assets which hardly put him on the breadline. In 1987, however, Nicholas went into a London hospital for tests and was given a clean bill of health. Seemingly a hypochondriac, he appeared relieved by the diagnosis.

The Crow's Nest, which looked out towards the Paternosters rocks and the island of Sark, was spacious and potentially stylish, but the Newalls lived in some domestic chaos and the place was usually untidy.

Roderick and Mark were brought up strictly by their parents. When they were young the nanny was employed and they were extremely careful in their choice of schools. The brothers began their education in the kindergarten at St Michael's in Jersey, but at the surprisingly young age of six and seven they were despatched to Lockers Park prep school at Hemel Hempstead in Hertfordshire as full time boarders. Later, at thirteen, they went to Radley College at Abingdon in Oxfordshire and remained there until they were seventeen and eighteen respectively. Nicholas, in particular, expected very high standards of achievement, and although he was keen for the boys to enjoy a wide range of sports he also tried to instil in them a love of learning. However, the wife of a local JP said that she felt 'they had a marvellous childhood, crammed full of activities and action'. She also strongly asserted that the Newalls were 'both good parents who did their best for their sons' and that there was 'nothing in their family life which could have been responsible for this tragedy'. She remembered that Roderick and Mark were greatly attached to their large mongrel dog Timmy who would follow them wherever they went 'endangering life and limb as he endeavoured to lick their faces as their surf boards hurtled to the shore at St Ouen's Bay, before going to share their hamburgers at one of the beachside cafés'.

Other reports disagree, stressing that although the Newall brothers were not unloved, little was done to make them feel needed. Maureen Ellam went even further, telling the *Daily Telegraph* that: 'They treated their sons so coldly that, if you treated your dog like that, you would be reported to the RSPCA. I don't think the boys ever had a kiss and a cuddle from their parents all their lives. Nick was utterly cold towards both boys. They did not exist to him, apart from white knuckles and real hate. They were four very different and volatile people.' Maureen Ellam went on to add that Nicholas referred to his sons as

'Elizabeth's boys'. Clearly he saw them as his wife's indulgence and were certainly unwanted by him.

Some of this problem is reflected in the recollections of a childhood friend who often played with the boys when they were young. He remembered them as 'perfectly normal kids' with whom he played on the beach, swimming, larking about. Their father, however, 'he was the lord. He ruled. He didn't shout or scream at them, and I never saw him hit them, but he had a bell; when he rang the bell it was time for them to come up to the house.'

The friend remembered Nicholas 'never used to come out to play with the boys and the house was not the sort of place where you play in the lounge'.

There seems no doubt that Nicholas always demanded a high degree of commitment from his sons. He introduced the boys to skiing, surfing, golf, scuba-diving, sailing and water-skiing and supplied them with all the necessary equipment, but in these, as in everything they undertook, he expected them to excel. Friends of the family noticed that both Roderick and Mark grew up to be highly competitive like their parents and in their younger days 'vied with each other in an almost excessive form of sibling rivalry'.

The childhood friend reflected that even as a child he noticed that 'they were not the tidiest family in the world. I would arrive sometimes at 9.30 in the morning and there would be no one up. It was not a dirty house, just untidy – dishes left on the draining board and that type of thing. They would not have picked things up until they had to. They knew Mum [their household help] was coming and it would get tidied up.

'I remember that Nicholas had a chair, a leather chair, I think it was a Parker Knoll, that was his pride and joy. I got the impression that they were comfortably off, far more comfortably off than we were, but the kids were not flashy with money, not at all. They [the boys] did not want for anything that I could see.'

The friend remembered that even at a young age the boys were knowledgeable about business matters. 'On one occasion Roderick lost a fishing rod but his immediate reaction was "Don't worry, we'll claim off the insurance."

'Roderick was bigger than his brother and me, and because of that seemed to dominate. Not to the extent of beating hell out of his brother, though. They seemed to get on well.'

In fact, Roderick and Mark, despite their rivalry, did have one bond; it was as if they were victims, sharing a common adversity, and this bonding had begun at an early age. Dominated and directed by Nicholas the boys had to fight hard to establish any identity of their own. They must have both felt appendages and could never really enter the close relationship between their mother and father.

The feeling of being outsiders persisted, and when they were young both Roderick and Mark must have felt that Nicholas and Elizabeth were not like other boys' parents. There was no sense of intimacy, no games with their father, who must have seemed light years away from them. Certainly life was well organised but everything was in sealed compartments – the sailing, the boarding schools, the lonely playing, the ring of the bell to summon the boys back to stand outside the walls of their parents' exclusive love for each other.

Everyone agrees that neither Roderick nor Mark ever lacked in any material way, but they must have soon realised that spiritually at least they were very much on their own. As a result there developed between them an inner bond of loyalty that was to produce a mutual reliance that was almost intuitive, almost 'twin'-like. In every other way, however, the two boys were considerably at odds with each other and would fight viciously. In fact, so bad was their relationship at Radley that they had to be sent home separately for the holidays.

Of the two Mark Newall, who became Head Boy, clearly felt most rejected by his parents and concealed his anguish under an increasingly cold, supercilious personality. He openly considered his parents 'grossly negligent and utterly incompetent' and a fellow pupil at Radley remembered him as unpopular, arrogant and extremely unpleasant. He told the *Telegraph* that Mark 'used to have fits of anger and punch holes through the plasterboard walls with his bare fist. I remember once he walked around with a leather strap wrapped around his fist because he was so scared of being set on. I think he was roughed up by the bigger boys when he first arrived and he never forgot it.' Mark, who had a very fine mind and was highly efficient, never forgot anything.

Roderick, on the other hand, covered up his parents' indifference to him by becoming a leader, a daredevil, a charismatic boy who was determined to draw attention to himself. He was an NCO in the Radley cadet force and had a clear ambition to join the army. He told his friends frankly the reason was that 'he wanted to kill people'. Tony Hudson, a house-master at Radley, said in an interview with the *Telegraph* that there was an atmosphere when Roderick and his parents were together and pointed out, 'To get the best out of school and enjoy it, there has to be teamwork between parents, teacher and boy. Maybe Roderick did not have the full teamwork.'

One ironic example of this is when Nicholas Newall arrived at a school sports day to film Roderick in a race. He seemed quite unable to recognise his son and pointed the camera at another fair-haired boy. Worse still, when

Nicholas became aware of his mistake, he simply handed the film to the other boy's family without having the grace to mention or apologise about the situation to Roderick. He must have found it difficult to bounce back after that one.

Nicholas Newall had aspirations to being a children's writer and wrote at least two manuscripts that remained unpublished. Perhaps because Elizabeth was seemingly so immature herself, he saw her as his child and there was no room for any more – particularly a couple of demanding and intelligent boys who might one day usurp his position in the home – or even with Elizabeth. So Nicholas used iron will to keep Roderick and Mark disciplined and at a distance.

The childhood friend remembered, 'Nicholas had an air of discipline about him, like a schoolmaster – a typical schoolmaster – academic with his own study where he worked. We never saw him when he was working.'

He did not feel the boys were subjected to harsh physical punishment. 'There was something, I can't remember if it was a cane, but their father would threaten [them] with it if they were caught. "Once more and you'll get it", sort of thing, but I can't remember what *it* was. I never saw them get it. It seemed to me to be normal parental discipline, rather like we would have "the naughty chair".'

Perhaps it would have been better if Nicholas *had* beaten his sons, for this would have indicated passion, anger and even the possibility of mutual warmth and recognition. At least there would have been some displayed emotion; instead Nicholas was an old-fashioned disciplinarian who, while not physically aggressive, could be witheringly sarcastic. It was an attitude that left both Roderick and Mark floundering.

The childhood friend continued, 'I'd say their mother

was loving towards them to a degree, but not over-protective. It was not hugs and kisses all the time. They had to look after themselves, but that, I think, was down to their boarding school. They could look after themselves from an early age. They did not strike me as being unusual.' He added slowly, 'They [Roderick and Mark] would almost certainly have played on the other side of Greve de Lecq, the side the bodies were found, although I don't remember playing there with them. Any child living down there would have known those woods.'

Ironically, Roderick, assisted by Mark, buried their parents in a spot they had known intimately from child-hood and which could easily be viewed from their old home.

Some family friends described Radley College, Oxford-shire, Roderick and Mark's public school, as 'a very fair school which embodies some of the best aspects of Chris-tian ethics', but unfortunately, it was felt, modern methods of education which require selection at the age of fourteen can lead to pupils ceasing to study such subjects as history and geography 'which, though not so obviously useful in the exam stakes and in earning a living, are invaluable in giving a more balanced view of life – giving an insight into the different consequences of moral and immoral behaviour in society.'

It was in fact observed that when they were older the boys seemed to have the attitude that 'information was only for the furtherance of wealth and power', but a child's earliest role model is without doubt its parents, and because Nicholas was so dominant his materialism must have rubbed off on to both Roderick and Mark.

Mark in particular had obviously learnt that if love wasn't readily available, then money was an essential reassuring replacement. He had watched his father's 'savings' system in action and this must have made him realise how important financial security was.

A visitor to the Newall household remembered Nicholas as highly autocratic, a man who was used to having every domestic task carried out for him, if rather vaguely and untidily, by Elizabeth. 'He was used to having people around . . . who would do things for him. There was a story, and I know it to be true, of how one lady who used to clean their house gave in her notice because Nicholas had asked her to clean his shoes. She told him that she didn't clean her husband's – he cleaned his own – and she certainly was not going to clean his. That was the end of that. Although he did not give the impression of being a wealthy man he must have come from a very wealthy family. He certainly gave you that impression. Elizabeth was the same. She obviously came from a wealthy background . . . They were used to the good things, the comfortable things of life.'

Certainly neither seemed aware of the idea of personal development, of being self-critical or of re-evaluating one's situation. The cushioning, although not that of millionaires, was too great. Nicholas and Elizabeth Newall had created their own comfortable little world in Jersey and in Spain and therefore, as people, marked time.

Once Roderick and Mark were at Radley, they were trained, as the British public school system intends its pupils to be trained, to become leaders, and in this they found little difficulty. Both were highly intelligent and capable, intellectually and physically. Roderick had always wanted to go into the army and the school was an ideal pre-training ground. Because of so much sailing experience, he had become very resourceful and Mark was much the same. The isolation of public school life, with its potential for great bouts of homesickness, and the spartan existence did not seriously worry either of them. The words 'clean-cut', 'fearless' and 'playing the game' were easily applicable to the Newall brothers. They were, without doubt, ostensibly 'muscular Christians'. Both good-looking, both charismatic, both rather grand and aloof, they were prototypes of 'leaders of men'. What is more, less confident and humbler spirits would have followed them anywhere – and there is equally no doubt that Roderick and Mark Newall led from the front. In this way, Nicholas and Elizabeth were very proud of their sons' careers at public school. However, the visitor comments, 'For most of the time, the impression I got of Nicholas – and Elizabeth to a certain extent – was that he was bothered about money. They seemed to live comfortably enough, and they certainly didn't spare it on the boys' education . . . but he would dream up the most silly ways of supposedly saving money. I remember him ringing me once to go to the Crow's Nest to have a look at something he had bought . . . it was a really nice mobile home, a camper. It was fitted out beautifully and I remarked that it would be splendid to take on holiday. He told me that he had not bought it primarily for that reason but because he was finding hotels too expensive when he and Elizabeth went across to England to visit Roderick and Mark at school at half-term. He didn't seem to realise that with the capital he had invested in this thing, and the cost of taking it across on the ferry to the UK, it probably would have been cheaper in the long run to continue staying in hotels, as they had always done. It was a strange sort of economic move.'

Strange, but typical of Nicholas's tunnel vision – a vision that Roderick also shared up to a point. Both father and son would strike out for an objective and go for it without realising the consequences or seeing the other options that lay along the path to their goal. Nan Clarke, Elizabeth's sister, told the *Telegraph*: 'Roderick is an extrovert, impulsive and very like his mother. Mark is more Machiavellian and resembles his father. Both are extremely clever and in a way completely amoral, as the younger generation tend to be because they haven't been brought up with a sense of social obligation. Roderick has never looked me in the eye since the murders. Mark can do so without any trouble. As a child, he could look me in the eye and lie. He was never one you could talk to. Their father, Nick, hadn't had a proper family upbringing. His mother and father travelled a lot and he was brought up by a nanny. I don't think he found fatherhood easy but he wasn't an unkind or uncaring father. Our two families shared many happy holidays. I think I knew Elizabeth's boys as well as I knew my own.'

'Elizabeth's boys' – the telling phrase is repeated again. Was Nicholas jealous of them? Was that why he kept such a tight reign on them and remained so aloof? Was the challenge Roderick and Mark presented so great that it made Nicholas retreat into illness?

By the time Roderick and Mark left Radley, they had become highly accomplished young men, with considerable abilities and potential, but they remained unloved and Roderick, the more emotionally demanding of the two, surely must have bitterly resented his father's domination, particularly when he saw the greater give and take of other families. This resentment could have turned into a slow-burning flame which no amount of material or status satisfaction would mask. He could recognise the loveless repression of his childhood and it only needed a chain of circumstances, another sign of rejection, to fan that flame into fire. Tragically the change was not going to be long in coming, and Nicholas would find that his eldest son's anger and resentment were a terrible force to be reckoned with.

Because of his unruly behaviour which largely consisted of bouts of attention-seeking daredevil showing off, Nicholas gave him a one-way ticket to Australia. But his wayward son was back in a few months. Elizabeth then sent him on an Outward Bound course in Scotland and then to Sandhurst.

One particular quality Roderick inherited from his parents was a love of the open air, of the sea and the challenge of becoming its master. Here his 'showing off' became resolution and his competence in a yacht was undoubted. One officer in the Royal Green Jackets commented that Roderick would either end up with the VC – or in prison. His army exploits were legion, and when stationed in Germany he set out to impress his peers by driving down the autobahn near Hamburg at 140 mph in foggy conditions, executing handbrake turns. On a more official level he was chosen for his regiment's winter expedition to St Moritz for the annual 'Swift and Bold' handicap. Roderick claimed to have descended the Cresta Run on a tea tray – a stunt that followed the recording of one of the fastest times on the run that year. Was he trying to prove that he was good enough to be his father's son – and not just one of 'Elizabeth's boys'.

Towards the end of his army career, Roderick made a short tour of Northern Ireland. He was promoted to Lieutenant and had his own platoon to command.

'There was a gap of four or five years when I did not see them,' the childhood friend reflected. 'I did not see Roderick after that, but I saw Mark when his parents were away in the Prince of Wales [the pub at the foot of the cliff below the Newalls' original house, the Crow's Nest]. Just to say hello, that sort of thing.

'He [Mark] had a Mini, a silver Mini. I think he would have bought that, rather than his father. He was then working in the finance industry, definitely a collar and tie job, because he would come in the Prince after work. I never saw him drunk.'

Mark appeared to have inherited his father's irritating air of superiority, but was much more talented. Despite the built-in advantage of finding a good financial post in a tax haven, he soon proved himself and became a fund manager. Because of the way the Newall brothers had had to rely on their own resources as children and because of the unique bond that had formed Mark's loyalty to Roderick was total despite their enmity. It was these qualities that were soon to be tested to the full.

Two visitors to the Crow's Nest at Greve de Lecq were a husband and wife who prefer to remain anonymous. The wife was the more frequent visitor of the two and saw Elizabeth regularly from the time the Newalls arrived in Jersey until they sold the house. The husband described Nicholas as a sergeant-major type, big and loud. 'He had a great, booming voice and gave the impression of being extremely arrogant. Elizabeth was more a sporting, sort of jolly hockey sticks, type.

'The stories about Nicholas summoning their sons from play with a school bell were true, but should not be misinterpreted,' he added, stating that the ringing 'was an easy way of telling the boys to return to the house and nothing more. It certainly was not a case of them not being able to return home until the bell was rung.' Neither did he ever see either Nicholas or Elizabeth striking them, but on the other hand they never saw them show the boys 'any sort of parental affection'.

The husband continued to reflect on the apparently loveless atmosphere at the Crow's Nest. 'When I say that the boys' upbringing was strange, what I mean to say is that it was strange to people like us. We have children and I'd like to think we showed them more affection than those boys were shown by their parents.

'They never went without, but they certainly weren't spoilt. If one of the boys wanted something, a bike or a fishing rod, for example, they were told that they could have it but it would be the next birthday or Christmas present. And Nicholas and Elizabeth stuck to that.'

His wife was in full agreement about the closeness of the Newall parents' relationship and he continued, 'Nicholas was dominant. Although he never laid a finger on either Roderick or Mark, he didn't have to. One word from him, in that booming voice, was enough. I wouldn't say that it was an unhappy household, but as far as the boys were concerned, it wasn't one in which they received a great deal of love and attention from their parents. If Nicholas said anything to either Roderick or Mark and the instruction wasn't obeyed immediately, they would be sent to their room.'

His wife added, 'There was very little in the way of what I would call normal physical contact between the boys and their parents, not even with Elizabeth. I have no doubt they looked after their children, but I have to question whether or not they really loved them. If they did then they certainly didn't show it a lot, and certainly not in front of me.'

The fact that there was so little outward display of affection and almost certainly a marked absence of demonstrative love seemed to have affected Roderick more than Mark, but then he appeared to be more emotionally demanding than his brother. Mark had already built his own defences and was determined to succeed on his own.

The wife also remembered how the Newall brothers

hated the thought of going back to boarding school and her recollection was that they had been sent there at a very early age. 'The boys, who were normal little boys, didn't appear to like it, and although I never saw them protest about the thought of going back to school, I could tell they weren't happy. It wasn't just a case of kids being sad that the holidays were over, I've seen that with my own children. This was something different.'

Her husband recalled that although Nicholas was big and loud, he didn't think he had a violent temper. 'I remember once taking my own son fishing and asking if they wanted to come too. They jumped at it and while we were there a couple of seasonal workers tried to muscle in when the three boys were fishing. Then one of them kicked one of the lads' rods, I think it was Roderick's, into the water. Knowing Nicholas as I did I thought he was going to go mad, because he was a strict disciplinarian, but when I took the lads home and explained what had happened, all he said was that they were insured for all that, and sure enough, a new rod was bought with the insurance money.'

His wife noticed that Nicholas and Elizabeth rarely took their sons out. 'Take fishing, for example – the boys came with my husband because he was taking our son. I don't think the reverse would have applied because Nicholas would not have taken the boys fishing. They might have gone fishing while they were on the boat, but the fishing was incidental to Nicholas . . . it was not the reason for taking the boat out.'

Looking back, her husband was sure Roderick and Mark were afraid of their father. 'They weren't terrified, they didn't live in fear of him, or anything like that, but he was very much the sergeant-major type and one word from him and they jumped.'

His wife underlined the aridity of the Newall brothers'

childhood. 'There's no doubt that both Nicholas and Eliza-beth wanted their boys to do well at school. The emphasis was always very much on education, even from quite a young age. They certainly were not allowed out to play until all their school work was done. They wanted the very best for their sons, and they saw that the only way they could achieve that was through education.'

The husband remembered seeing Nicholas on the day he was murdered. 'We were driving and saw him and Mark together, in the van the police said had been hired for Mark to move into his new home. They were about a couple of miles from where Mark's new house was. As far as we could see Roderick wasn't with them although he may well have been in the back of the van. They both saw us and waved.'

The wife continued, 'When Nicholas and Elizabeth were in Spain, and Mark was living in the chalet alongside Crow's Nest, he was handling all the financial affairs, as far as I could make out. He used to handle everything when they were away, and after the boys left school they were away for most of the time.'

Her husband said, 'I'm very surprised that Roderick would have even thought about raising his hand to his father. Nicholas was a big man. I am not small but I would certainly have thought twice about tackling Nicholas.

'I know the field in which the bodies were found. I drive past there several times a week. The boys used to play there when they were younger. I'm surprised that the bodies were found there. I always thought that they would be found somewhere near where Nicholas and Elizabeth lived, but not on that side of Crow's Nest, more on the other side, where the police found the remains of stuff that was burnt. We have seen some of what remained from that fire. We didn't recognise it as coming from Crow's

Nest. There were aerosol cans that I think were manufactured, or certainly bought, in Spain.

'To people like us, the boys' upbringing was a strange one. But thinking about it, people like Nicholas and Elizabeth would think it a perfectly normal one . . . They were very, very strict parents . . . As the years went on, after Nicholas and Elizabeth were reported missing, the feeling I had that the boys were somehow involved in their disappearance grew stronger. I think the whole island knew it, well, they didn't know it, but they certainly suspected it. It was talked about quite openly.'

Finally, the wife concluded, 'I didn't believe it, not even when people were talking about it. I refused to believe that any son could be involved in the death of his mother. I didn't even believe it after Roderick was arrested in his boat. It was only when he pleaded guilty after obviously showing the police where the bodies were buried that I thought it could be true. Even now, it's difficult to think about.'

The main contention in Roderick Newall's murder of his parents was the extent of alleged premeditation, and there are various clues that could support the possibility either way. On one hand, he was carefully trained by the army in evolving a strategy to deal with the enemy in as effective and economic a way as possible. It would have been quite conceivable to evolve a strategy for murdering his parents, particularly in the light of events to come. Careful planning could conclude in the total disappearance of Nicholas and Elizabeth, rather as if they had never existed. Because of so much lonely play, he knew every inch of the countryside around his former home at the Crow's Nest.

Alternatively, his emotions, already running high in gathering resentment, only needed to be fuelled even further to burst into flame. The idea of *crime passionnel* is therefore also a distinct possibility. Nicholas had taught his son to live without love, but in order to do this a ruthless cynicism must grow. Roderick Newall was no monster, but his tunnel vision could well have been about to produce an increasing obsession with his father's dominance.

In early 1987, with both their sons away from home, Nicholas and Elizabeth decided to move to a smaller house. The Crow's Nest was too big for them now and Nicholas, always anxious to save money, decided to buy a modest bungalow a short distance away in Clos de l'Atlantique. The sea view was obscured by the proximity of other buildings and the outlook was suburban and dull-looking – a far cry from the beautiful position of their former home – but because they spent so much time in Javea, perhaps the Newalls felt they had had enough of the sea.

As a result of the move, Nicholas and Elizabeth formed a strong friendship with the couple who bought the Crow's Nest, David and Maureen Ellam. Although the friendship was short-lived it was intense and David Ellam remembers, 'They were fabulous people to spend time with. It's very difficult to get four people who get on together and we did. Though we were all different in many ways, we all clicked as a foursome.'

After the Newalls' disappearance it was David and Maureen Ellam who fought for a murder investigation, and had it not been for them and other friends who kept the pressure up and maintained the link between other members of the family and the Jersey police, it is unlikely that any arrests would have been made.

Of Nicholas, David Ellam commented, 'He suffered the

problem that a lot of reasonably educated people suffer from, and I'm conceited enough to put myself in this category, in that you don't find enough sensible, in-depth conversation in your normal man. He [Nicholas] was easily bored with people. With the Newalls we had a common link there. I could talk to him about sailing because he knew about sailing and I was interested. We did not talk about inane things which is what most men talk about.'

Nicholas Newall, because of his private income, had created his own world and mode of existence. Living modestly, he could continue his life of comparative ease in Jersey and Spain for as long as he could foresee. This meant that he could pick and choose the people he wanted to know as well as the activities and interests he wished to undertake. As a result, none of his hard edges had been rubbed off by meeting people he *didn't* get on with – say, in a working environment – and therefore he would not indulge in the cut and thrust of debate or take any criticism. It is true that he worked in some of the island's schools, but the abrasive – or even openly hostile – atmosphere of the staffroom was unlikely to reach him for he knew that if he wanted to leave he could because of his private income. Nicholas Newall was himself an island.

2

Roderick and Mark Newall's careers as army officer and fund manager respectively got off to a good start and seemed to be progressing favourably. Both had a promising future in terms of promotion, but Roderick probably found at quite an early stage that the army was not dissimilar to being back in his father's house. Both were strict institutions, both provided security, but both were relentless imprisoners of the emotions. They had to be. It was part of Nicholas's make-up to be a leader, partly perhaps because he felt increasingly insecure as his sons grew to manhood. He had done little with his life and was no doubt wondering if Roderick and Mark were going to do a good deal more with theirs – putting him in the lotus-eating shade.

Slowly, Roderick may well have begun to draw comparisons between the two institutions and possibly to dislike them equally, nursing romantic ideas of sailing away somewhere remote and opening a boat-chartering business – possibly in South America or the Falklands – but the very thought of approaching his stringent father and asking for his backing was ludicrous. Nicholas's tyranny was absolute. He was proud of his son's army career and would never have tolerated a change of this kind; he would have seen the move as a loss of respectability and ambition, as well as a breach of discipline. When the time came for Roderick officially to resign his commission, his father would have seen him taking up a management job where his skills as an officer could still be used. But not until then. What was more, Nicholas must have liked to dine out on Roderick's career as much as Mark's; so far his obedient sons had come up to scratch.

It would be wrong to paint a picture of Nicholas as a monster, but without doubt he was both a tyrant and a bigot where 'duty' was all and the physical, more emotional expressions of love were locked away somewhere deep inside him. Even Elizabeth would never have questioned Nicholas's attitude to their sons.

In fact, according to her sister, Nan Clarke, Elizabeth was very pleased at the success of her two sons. She remembered how happy she was in May 1987 when 'Roderick was introduced to his Commander-in-Chief, Princess Alexandra, while we were attending a reception in Whitehall. She was equally delighted that Mark had taken on the chore of looking after their finances and proud of the success he was having with his chosen career.'

Maureen Ellam commented to the *Telegraph* however, 'The boys watched their parents go through their inheritance and even sell this house, which had great potential, and buy one which had nothing. I see many rich people on this island. The idea is that if you inherit something, you tend to add to it and pass it on to your children. Nick and Elizabeth were not like that. When money came to them, it was the end of the line.'

Roderick's restlessness as an army officer must have slowly grown, but it was not until his great uncle decided to make such a substantial donation to his parents' income that his longing for another life – and the money that would finance it – might be said to have crystallised. Soon he could think of nothing else but buying his freedom – just as his father had done when he had set off from Scotland to the West Indies so many years ago with his young family. Roderick had dim but poignant memories of that trip, and even if the voyage had terminated at Jersey's attractive tax haven, it still symbolised the great escape. Wind slapping on sail, the endless vista of sea, the hope of landfall, a new life – and a departure from the predictable rigours of the army. It would all have been so immensely fulfilling – had not his father been his jailer.

Mark's career turned out to be more personally satisfying. For a young man of twenty, he had done exceptionally well and was now a Eurobond dealer at Sheppard's, working for the BAII (Banque Arabe et Internationale d'Investissements), whose offices are on the Esplanade at St Helier. In October 1987, however, he had only just returned to work in Jersey, having been based at the firm's London office. Although Mark was academically bright, it must be made clear that as the island's main business is finance, many young men and women are able to work themselves into particularly good jobs there. He was well paid, had recently bought himself a house called La Falaise at nearby Noirmont and, unlike his brother, was looking forward to an excellent future in a job he enjoyed.

Roderick must have confided some of his dissatisfaction to Mark, who was sympathetic and no doubt felt as strongly about Nicholas's domination as Roderick did. Mark must also have been able to sense the link between Roderick's and his father's personality, understand the thrusting tyranny. They wanted to have their own way, Nicholas and Roderick; they *had* to.

Once, when Maureen Ellam commented to Roderick

on how much like his mother he was, he had replied, 'It's funny we look this way because we're the other way about as people. I'm more like father and Mark's like mother.'

Opinions here differ. Although everyone agrees that Roderick looked very like his mother – 'You looked at him and saw Elizabeth,' one friend said simply – few felt that Mark had inherited his mother's nature. Roderick in fact was the gregarious one, hot-tempered and a brilliant sportsman – 'impetuous and extrovert like his mother,' another friend concurred. She added, 'Mark was introverted, serious and Machiavellian like his father.'

A loner at school where he seemed to have few close friends, in later life Mark still seemed to prefer his own company, and although he was often alone it was felt that this was usually from choice.

'Roderick, encouraged by his father, who was a very keen and competent sailor, learned to love the sea and sailing as much as Nicholas, and they often sailed together,' a friend commented. 'On one occasion, I remember them taking *Chanson du Lecq* through the French canals with Bridget, his girlfriend. He spent many holidays in Javea, sailing, wind-surfing and scuba-diving.'

The same source revealed that although Mark was equally keen on sport a knee injury made him selective. During his teens he was very interested in martial arts. When he became old enough to remain on his own on Jersey, Mark Newall did not go to Spain. She felt that Mark, who 'rarely drank alcohol and was the master of self-control, was very quiet and a bit cold.' She also stated that the Newall brothers were both highly competitive. In her opinion it was only in the summer of 1987 that they became close friends and regularly sought out each other's company. 'They were both quite single-minded,' she said, 'with a total disdain for authority especially when it tried to impede what they wanted to do. Mark would listen, look at you, as though you could not understand. Roderick would smile, agree, and then both would go ahead with what they wanted to do. They were always willing politely to listen to the arguments, but quite secure in their superior knowledge.' However, she did add, 'In spite of this, they are both capable of intense loyalty to friends and, given the choice of betraying their country or their friends, the country would not be considered worthy of consideration.'

Other friends on the island stated that Roderick had 'raised a hand' to his mother in an argument some seven months before her death. These friends saw the Newalls as 'very positively self-willed and independent people, who were bound to clash with each other and themselves'. They described Nicholas as 'an intensely interesting man who didn't suffer fools gladly, was argumentative, but was immensely fair and not petty.' They said, 'He dealt in verbal ... pugilistics, not physical aggressiveness,' but they felt he could be insensitive to other people's feelings.

'Both Roderick and Mark,' a friend commented, 'had considerable affection for their extended family, particularly their maternal grandmother ... I think that one of the things that has upset them most is the way this tragedy has affected the family and caused them to become outcasts ... I believe it was in the hope of repairing this breach that Roderick so bravely went to see his uncle.' This event took place some five years after the murder of his parents.

The terms of Kenneth Newall's pre-decease gift became clear in mid-September 1987, just a few weeks before

Nicholas and Elizabeth were murdered, and the matter was discussed when the Newalls went to Sark to see Kenneth some days after they had returned to Jersey from Spain. They came home in very high spirits indeed and went to London where Elizabeth, under Nicholas's benign eye, had a shopping spree in Harrods. Now the constraints of living on a fixed income had been removed, they could, at last, undertake some cautious spending. A friend commented, 'It was noticeable after Elizabeth and Nick learnt that his Uncle Kenneth had changed his will, that she was spending more money on things like clothes and shopping in places like Harrods and seemed to burst with radiance and dress better.'

In his will, Kenneth Newall left nothing to either Nicholas or his twin brother, Stephen. Instead, he made their children sole beneficiaries, subject to the following proviso: one-sixth of the total estate was to go to Stephen's children and one-sixth to Nicholas and Elizabeth's sons, 'in equal shares absolutely'. He also instructed that the remaining two-thirds be converted into cash and the interest income paid to Gertrude Beattie of Troon, Ayrshire and Dorothy Gordon Campbell of Bearsden, Glasgow, in equal shares during their lives. On the death of either Gertrude or Dorothy, one-half of the capital, and on the death of the survivor, the remainder of the capital, 'shall be paid to the children of the said Stephen Paul Newall and Nicholas Park Newall in equal shares absolutely'.

Later, Gertrude Beattie stated that the income she received did *not* represent a large sum, so the bulk of the money was obviously the cash gift, no doubt to avoid considerable inheritance tax, made to Stephen and Nicholas.

* * *

39

Nicholas and Elizabeth had always been close to Kenneth, or 'Uncle Sark' as Elizabeth affectionately referred to him, and on 21st November 1987, a month after the Newalls' 'disappearance', Kenneth died from a coronary.

It is possible that in desperation Roderick did plead with his parents to finance him to leave the army at this time, and perhaps that is the reason the Newalls were so upset when they saw Maureen Ellam on the fateful morning of 10th October, and said that they would have to spend more time on Jersey.

There is also a possibility that Roderick decided the only way to buy his freedom was to destroy not only authority but the financial deadlock. Was it possible that at this stage he might well have thought of killing his parents? Could he have started to plan the attack with military precision? The problem he was facing was that if he defied his father and left the army of his own volition he would have no money and no job worth having – and the romantic dream of the exotic yacht charter business would be as far away as ever.

This, of course, is only surmise. The other possibility is that his murder of Nicholas and Elizabeth was a spur-of-the-moment decision, the result of an argument while singularly drunk, with the alcohol cementing and enlarging the intense hatred that could have built up in Roderick over the years.

On the evening of Friday, 9th October, both brothers returned to Jersey unexpectedly, Roderick at 8 p.m. and Mark at 8.30 p.m., staying together at Mark's new house which was still barely furnished. They did not see their parents but phoned them to say that they were going to take them out to dinner at the Sea Crest the next evening to celebrate Elizabeth's birthday. Perhaps Roderick also said that he wanted to talk about 'money' or the future, and that was another reason why the Newalls seemed so upset when they went round to see the Ellams at 10 a.m. on the morning of Saturday, 10th October. They could well have needed contact and discussion and reassurance, but clearly, neither Nicholas nor Elizabeth could bring themselves to admit that their son might be putting pressure on them over the squalid subject of finance. Having always described Roderick's and Mark's careers as such a great success, it would have been impossible to break the habit of a lifetime.

Elizabeth's was the most mysterious comment of the entire case – that they would be spending more time on the island. The Ellams were delighted and Maureen remembered saying that they would be able to have two dinner parties a week – one at the Crow's Nest and the other at Clos de l'Atlantique. Despite the lightness of the conversation, the Newalls stayed for two hours, deriving considerable comfort from the Ellams. Elizabeth also told Maureen, 'You'll never guess what – the boys are coming over today for my birthday dinner.' This was a clear indication that they had no idea the boys were already on the island. Nicholas and Elizabeth had also been busy preparing to return to Spain; the plan was that they would depart on 20th October and return to Jersey on 18th December 1987.

As Maureen Ellam was wondering what was wrong with the usually buoyant Newalls, it was later discovered by the police that a man had visited Norman's Builders Merchants in St Helier that morning and spent £103.42p on two trenching spades, one green plastic tarpaulin and one blue, two torches and batteries, two packets of red heavy duty refuse sacks, a pick axe, two small modelling knives,

41

a saw, rope and a can of upholstery cleaner. Similar tarpaulins and red refuse sacks were later found wrapped around the bodies of Nicholas and Elizabeth Newall when their bodies were exhumed in November 1993. Later, the assistant could only describe the purchaser as 'tall and Germanic looking'. While that is similar to the description of Roderick Newall, with his sweeping mop of blond hair and heroic Teutonic features, on the other hand witnesses have failed to recognise him from photographs.

In fact, the confusion was due to a strange and perplexing coincidence. Along with the tarpaulins, police claim, Roderick also bought a grubbing tool which had an eight centimetre cutting edge, similar in size to an injury found by pathologists on the back of Nicholas Newall's head. This grubbing tool was never found. The police naturally believed that this gave them a lead but the saleswoman, Tina Collins, was unable positively to pick out Roderick's photograph from eleven others in an identity exercise as during the same month as Nicholas and Elizabeth Newall were murdered, a man named Sigurdur Hafsteinsson who resembled Roderick went to Norman's several times and was served by Miss Collins at least twice, on one of these occasions buying a tarpaulin.

In July the following year when Hafsteinsson went into Normans again, Tina Collins called the police to say that the man she thought had purchased the consignment of tarpaulins and the grubbing tool they were interested in was back in the shop. Mr Hafsteinsson was interviewed, found to be slightly older than Roderick but generally like him in appearance. He had bought a tarpaulin similar to the ones they believed Roderick had purchased and was eliminated from enquiries.

Both the Newall brothers, however, have always insisted that the tarpaulins and tools they used to conceal and bury the bodies were found by them at the bungalow after Roderick had killed his parents – another argument on the side of *crime passionnel*.

At 1 p.m., Roderick and Mark arrived at their parents' bungalow. Mark and Nicholas left immediately to pick up a hired van so that Mark could later use it to transport furniture from his temporary base at St John to his new home. In fact this was to be Nicholas and Elizabeth's unofficial hearse. They then went back to the bungalow for lunch and, later, the brothers returned to Noirmont.

That evening, Mark drove Roderick to Clos de l'Atlantique, arriving at the pre-arranged time of 8 p.m. There, the Newalls began the celebration with two valedictory bottles of champagne and Mark, being the most moderate drinker, drove the family to the Sea Crest restaurant. Nicholas wore a blue suit with a faint check while Elizabeth wore a cream high-necked blouse with frills on the cuffs and a red or possibly an orange skirt. The atmosphere was superficially buoyant, but it is possible that feelings were already running deep.

The Newall family arrived at the Sea Crest restaurant at Petit Port, St Brelade, between 9 and 9.30 p.m. and remained there until between 12 and 12.30 a.m. Roderick later told the police that another bottle of champagne was consumed at the restaurant before dinner and wine and liqueurs followed. The Newalls then returned to 9 Clos de l'Atlantique in Nicholas's silver Citroën. At the bungalow Roderick, Nicholas and Elizabeth began to drink an eighteen-year-old Macallan malt whisky. The fatal process of the loosening of tongues and inhibitions was beginning. What was more, the recent bequest from Uncle Sark was not only making the miserly Nicholas more financially reckless but it was allowing the family to drink with unnatural abandon, which no doubt permitted Roderick's highly charged feelings of childhood anger to seep through. For the first time in his life, he desperately needed the freedom he had never had under the triple regimes of his parents' loveless rule, boarding school and the army – three institutions that had regulated and imprisoned him for years, inhibiting his spirit of freedom.

At the committal proceedings in the police court in Jersey on Thursday, 17th March 1994, a statement written by Mark Newall at the island's La Moye prison three days before was read out. In this statement he said:

'My brother and parents drank a great deal of alcohol. They drank champagne before dinner and several bottles of wine at dinner. On returning to the house, they started on the whisky and started to argue, not violently, about my brother's career and other matters. It was an argument I had heard before. I was sober and not interested in the argument and therefore I went home.'

When Roderick Newall arrived back in Jersey in November 1993, having been extradited from Gibraltar after a fifteen-month legal battle following his arrest at sea, he made a statement to the police, under caution, which gives his version of the macabre events of that celebratory night of 10th October 1987.

'I admit that I killed my parents . . . My recollection is not completely clear after so much time. Briefly the circumstances were that, after Mark left, my parents and I were alone in the house and continued talking and drinking in the sitting-room of their home.'

But then the rumbling thunder of the familiar dispute that Mark had walked away from broke out into a violent confrontation between father and son.

'A heated argument developed,' continued Roderick in his statement to the police which was later read out in court 'in which many old wounds were reopened. It came to a head with my father and I standing face to face. I told him what I thought about him, things I had never said before. He pushed me. I fell hitting my head on the dining-room table. I fell on to a box of my possessions that I had taken out of the attic. On top of the box was a pair of rice flails [a weapon used in martial arts] which I grabbed and used to club my father. I remember him falling.'

Roderick Newall's statement continued: 'My next memory was finding myself sitting on the floor of the hall. I got up and went into the sitting-room and saw my father's body. I could feel no pulse. In complete panic, I checked the kitchen and the bedroom where I found my mother's body. It triggered my memory of also attacking her. I could find no pulse. Then I realised I had killed both my parents.'

In fact the Crown allege that Roderick planned the double killing to inherit Uncle Sark's bequest. Was it possible that he had so little love for his arid parents that he could plot such cold-blooded barbarity? Either way, however, *crime passionnel* or calculated murder, Nicholas Newall had dominated his life and to strike him down, whether drunkenly or cold sober, was to strike a blow for freedom. But Roderick was not to escape from his father's influence so easily; that iron, narrow will was to continue to dominate his life for the next seven years.

At the time, however, contemplating the bloody carnage he had created, Roderick must have felt in complete despair. His statement continued, 'Sometime later I contacted Mark and told him what had happened and told him the only thing for me to do was to kill myself.'

Mark's statement read, 'Some hours later, I was contacted by Roderick. He was crying and incoherent and stated that he had killed my mother and father in a drunken row and was going to kill himself. He kept saying he was sorry.'

Roderick corroborated this. 'He persuaded me not to and said he would meet me at the house. When Mark arrived, I was in the sitting-room, holding the shotgun.' The gun belonged to Nicholas.

Mark continued, 'I went straight to my parents' house and found my mother and father both dead. They had had serious head injuries. My brother had blood on him and was crying and in a distressed state, holding my father's shotgun. I told my brother that the best thing to do was to call the police. There was nobody else in the house. He said he would shoot himself. He felt the police would not understand the circumstances. I argued with him for some time and eventually I agreed to help conceal the crime. It was then, and is now, my belief that if I had not done this, he would have killed himself.'

Blood was splashed all over the two rooms and there was no doubt that if the two bodies were to be removed and the rooms cleaned up, the brothers would have to move fast before dawn came and the island woke.

But already Nicholas had lain on the sitting-room floor a sufficient length of time to allow the blood from his fractured skull to soak through both carpet and underlay to the floor below. Elizabeth had allegedly fallen to her knees after the first blow and probably died in that position. Like Nicholas, she lay there for a sufficient length of time for her blood to soak into the parquet floor below, and specks of blood were also found on the bedside lamp.

Now the decision had been made to remove and conceal the bodies, Mark went to find some materials to wrap them in. He stated, 'I found in the boiler room, garage and garden shed tarpaulins, tools and other equipment to clean the house and dispose of the evidence. There were several pairs of rice flails on the floor. Roderick gathered them up and I didn't see them. Roderick said he had cut them up and disposed of them.'

Wrapping their parents' bodies in the tarpaulins, the Newalls carried them cautiously out of the bungalow and, making sure they were unobserved, dumped them in the back of the van that was more than justifying its hire.

Roderick had already told the head of the murder enquiry, Detective Inspector Martin Fitzgerald, how he and Mark almost blundered badly during the disposal of the bodies. He said that he had been forced to reverse around a bend when he overshot the place chosen for burial – the field near the sea and the surfing beach where the two brothers had played as children. Roderick realised that he had driven too far when he saw the lights of some buildings.

Fitzgerald was therefore able to tell the court, 'Then he and Mark removed the bodies from the van and rolled them over the bank. Roderick then drove the van to the bottom of the hill, parked up and returned to the top to assist Mark in moving the bodies across the field to the burial site.'

The brothers then dug a grave that was 2 feet 3 inches deep; one report suggested that they buried their parents on top of each other, in head to toe position, wrapped in the tarpaulins.

Roderick's statement to the court read: 'Mark eventually calmed me down and talked me out of taking my life. Mark and I then took my parents in the hired van and buried them. We then returned home and tried to remove all traces of what had happened.'

But the desperate hours attempting to clean the bunga-low were not nearly long enough, and this was to be the

Newalls' first mistake. Although they furiously scrubbed carpets and washed a duvet, stains still remained in the bedroom and on the floors. In order to speed up the process of drying out, the central heating was turned up, over-riding a thermostat control and remaining permanently on high. Later, Roderick was to burn some of his parents' possessions in an area of land known as La Vallette, close to the old Newall family home, the Crow's Nest, but it was not until 8th March 1988, five months later, that police dog handlers found debris from the actual seat of the fire in a nearby clearing. Other items were scattered over a large area around the fire. A partially burnt hand-bag, found in undergrowth and covered by leaves, was discovered to belong to Elizabeth Newall and contained a personalised Sheaffer pen with the name *J Hepburn*. This was later identified by a family friend, James Hepburn, who remembered giving her the pen in Belgium in May 1987.

The bag also contained cosmetics that Elizabeth was known to use. Amongst the burnt debris were lenses pre-scribed to Nicholas Newall in Andorra, Spain, on 17th June 1985, the remains of his pipe as well as two books. One of these, *Bouquet de France* by Samuel Chamberlain, was a cookery book and the handwriting inside was identi-fied by members of the Newall family as Elizabeth's. It had been a gift from her mother, Sheilah.

The most crucial evidence, however, involved a number of items that had very likely been used to clean up after the murders. The first was a spray upholstery cleaner with a brush attachment from which forensic experts later iden-tified tufts of fibres that matched the carpets in both lounge and bedroom of 9 Clos de l'Atlantique. Partially burnt and melted green and blue plastic was found and this was later identified as the same type as the tarpaulins that were bought at Norman's Builders Stores on 10th October 1987. Burnt pieces of green and white material were also present, and there was no significant difference between this material and the J-cloths in the kitchen at the Newalls' bungalow and the fibres found in the areas that had been cleaned.

Some distance from the fire, an iron bar was discovered which was 12 inches in length and about 1 inch in diameter. It had four metal links to one end. Although it was not known at the time if this was connected with the case, it was also exhibited.

More significantly a spade was later found in undergrowth on Noirmont Common – a spade that was identical to the two that had been bought at Norman's on 10th October and was actually still marked with the firm's price sticker. Nevertheless, despite all this incredible carelessness, there was still insufficient evidence with which to arrest the Newall brothers.

The bodies of Nicholas and Elizabeth Newall were buried fully clothed. In a further statement to the police, Roderick admitted that he 'had been responsible for setting fire to evidence which had been destroyed at Greve de Lecq after the murders. Burnt in the fire were personal items and those used to clean the house.' Asked if one of the items at the scene of the fire could have been one of the weapons used in the murders, he had said that this was possible.

At last Roderick was free of his father's tyranny, but for the moment all he must have felt was shock. Perhaps, however, in his subconscious mind, Roderick wanted that tyranny back. Could he really cope without it?

3

Elizabeth Newall's closest friend, Maureen Ellam, left the Crow's Nest at 8.45 a.m. on the morning of 11th October, to collect her brother from the airport. She, too, had had a birthday and received a large number of flowers, so she decided that she would give one of her bouquets to Elizabeth, dropping it in at the bungalow, along with a plant and a mosquito-killer that Nicholas had recently lent her. When Maureen Ellam arrived at 9 Clos de l'Atlantique she noticed two vehicles parked outside – Nicholas Newall's Citroën and Mark's white Toyota. She rang the bell, decided it was too early to socialise and was about to return to her car when Roderick opened the door. There was some routine conversation and he told her that his parents were still asleep. Ironically, Maureen Ellam then replied, 'Still asleep? Lay these on her bed. When she opens her eyes, she'll think she's dead.'

Maureen remembered that she 'went away alarmed. Still asleep? I thought. They wouldn't be asleep. Why did that boy [Roderick] tell me they were still asleep? And I thought, well, perhaps he should take them a cup of tea. Perhaps Nick was snoring. No, much more like, he didn't know me very well and I've come in a bit bouncy, with him thinking it was his duty to keep a stranger out of his parents' bedroom. I asked him what the time was and he said, "Nine o'clock." I said, "I blooming hope it's not much more because I've got to be at the airport at five past." "Okay, 'bye then," he said, and I drove off. All this was going through my mind as I was driving.'

Later, Roderick Newall stated as follows:

'We returned to my parents' house quite late. It was after midnight. Once there, we opened a bottle of the whisky that I had purchased earlier and had a few more drinks. Approximately one or two hours later Mark and I returned to Mark's house at La Falaise in the van. When we left, mum and dad were still up but preparing for bed. Mum had dozed off a bit earlier. It was a late night for mum and dad as they would normally retire between 10 pm and 11 pm unless they were entertaining.

'On the morning of Sunday 11 October 1987 I arose quite early. It was about 8 am. Mark wasn't up yet, but I could hear noises coming from his room. I had a shower and at about 8.20 am to 8.30 am Mark and I drove to mum and dad's in the MR2, which we had managed to start by bumping it. We arrived at the house. There was no sign of any activity. We entered the premises through the door which leads into the kitchen. The door was locked, but both Mark and I have keys, but I don't recall who opened the door. We went in and found both mum and dad asleep in bed. I think mum rolled over and said something, but I'm not sure. Dad as a rule is a very early riser, but I didn't think it strange after the previous night. Mark said: "Let them sleep it off", or something along those lines. We then left the bedroom and went to the kitchen for some breakfast. I can't remember if I had a bowl of cereal or not, but I did have some coffees. At about 9 am someone came to the door. I answered the door. I didn't know at the time who the lady was, but I now know her to be Mrs Ellam. She had a bouquet of flowers which she gave me for mum. Apparently it was her birthday the day before, and she had had too many flowers. She said: "These are for your mum; you can wake her up with them." This she said because I had told her that mum was still asleep in bed. Mrs Ellam didn't stay, as she left saying that she had to collect someone from the Airport. I then went into the bedroom and put the flowers by mum's bed, which woke her up. Dad was also starting to stir. I then left the bedroom and went into the sitting-room, or kitchen. A short while later dad came into the kitchen. There was no sort of conversation between Mark, dad or me, just good morning out of the head, that sort of thing. Dad made some breakfast. I don't know what, and I think he must have also made breakfast for mum. Both mum and dad were a bit under the weather, probably from the night before. At about 10 am Mark and I left my parents' house, making arrangements to return for lunch. Both mum and dad were in the kitchen, I think doing the dishes. Mark and I then returned to La Falaise with the car. There we put the mattresses which belonged to a lodger of the house into the van. We then returned to my parents' house for lunch. When we arrived, I think mum was in the kitchen and I think dad was in the sitting-room reading the Sunday papers. This was before midday. We sat down for lunch at around 12.30 pm to 1 pm. I was sitting oppo-site mum, Mark was opposite dad, and I have a feeling was beside me. I had for lunch Parma ham. Then mum, dad and Mark had smoked salmon. We all had scampi. We also drank a couple of bottles of wine. I don't remem-ber much of the conversation during lunch, but we spoke about Kenneth and family matters in general. I don't recall any visitors or phone calls during lunch. After lunch Mark and I did the dishes. I think I may have dried a couple of pots. Dad was in the sitting-room and mum was just sort of floating around. At about 3 pm, time was getting on, as Mark and I had to sort out this mattress before catching our flights. We left my parents' house and drove up to Mark's previous home.'

He then described how he and Mark off-loaded a mattress at Mark Newall's previous home in St John and how ultimately he took the hire van back to the premises at Falles Hire Cars at the Airport and how he caught a flight to England at 5.45 pm that evening.

In his statement Mark Newall stated as follows:

'We left the Seacrest about 12, quarter past, and returned to my parents' house where they all continued to drink. The highlight of the evening was when my mother had words with the head waiter over the colour of her lobster. Also there were words between my mother and Roderick over Roderick leaving the Army. Sometime after 2.30 in the morning I left my parents' home with Roderick. All by this time were well under the influence of drink and were falling asleep. We went back to La Falaise. It must have been about 3 o'clock because I looked at my watch before going to bed. The next morning, Sunday 11 October 1987, I woke up about 6 o'clock and at about 7.30 to 8 o'clock I got up as I was hungry. Roderick was up by about 8.15. As I had no milk, we decided to go to my parents for breakfast. We arrived there about 8.30. I let myself in by the back door. My parents were still in bed, so we made ourselves something to eat. About 9 o'clock Mrs Ellam came around with some flowers for my mother. Roderick went to the door while I stayed in the lounge. Roderick then took the flowers through to my mother. My parents then got up and dressed. I can't remember if my father went for the newspaper, but I remember him talking about it. At about 10 am Roderick and I went back to La Falaise in the car to collect a mattress and take it in the van. We returned in the van to my parents' house, where we arrived back for lunch. We had lunch, during which my parents and Roderick had white wine. During this time there were no problems, just normal conversation. Roderick and I left later than we meant to – about 3 o'clock. When I left my parents, all appeared in order.'

He too spoke of taking bedding back to his old home in St John, and taking the hire van back to the garage, and said that he caught a later flight than his brother, at 6.20 pm.

As Roderick and Mark Newall sat back in their separate aircraft, the sense of shock and incredulity must have spread inside them even more strongly than before. They would never see their parents again. Those familiar figures were lying battered in an unconsecrated, unmarked grave. Nicholas and Elizabeth Newall's perfect marriage was at an end, but Roderick and Mark must have pondered over their cups of airline coffee, would this be the perfect crime? Roderick, possibly with an appalling hangover, might still not remember much about the actual killings, but the question was, could the murder of Nicholas and Elizabeth Newall have been a spur-of-the-moment drunken assault, or was it the result of a carefully laid plan eventually to inherit Uncle Sark's bequest? Could the hatred Roderick may well have felt for their dominating father have resulted in him planning a strategy? Or did the hasty, amateur, bungled clean-up operation imply a family row leading to a drunken murder?

There is no doubt that Roderick would not have become a suspect had it not been for Maureen and David Ellam's tireless campaign to discover what had happened to their friends. Maureen was particularly concerned that she had not heard from the normally extremely communicative Elizabeth for at least two days. Naturally, she tried to call her but there was no reply. By the Wednesday, she had assumed that the Newalls had gone to stay with Kenneth Newall on Sark, but when she had still not heard from them by Thursday – the actual date of Elizabeth's forty-eighth birthday when they were all going to dine together in a restaurant in St Helier – her suspicions rose. Elizabeth would not have let her close friends down like this, not unless some urgent and unexpected business had come up on Sark or somewhere else. And even if it had, then, surely, she would have phoned.

Maureen's increasing anxiety was interrupted by the forces of nature; on the night of Thursday, 15th October, the great hurricane that was to cause millions of pounds' worth of damage on the mainland of the UK struck Jersey with equal ferocity. Although no one was killed, hundreds of trees fell and roofs were torn off. The devastation extended the time the Newalls' disappearance could pass without undue worry and Maureen, still seeking rational reasons for their absence, assumed they were unable to join them for dinner because of the storm and that now their telephone lines must be out of order.

But on Saturday, Maureen rang the Newalls' next-door neighbour, Mitchell Shearer, who told her that not only was there a hole in the Newalls' roof but their car had been parked outside the bungalow all week. Considerably alarmed now, Maureen asked Shearer to go and see if the Newalls were at home and he complied. Not being able to get a response from knocking at the front door, Shearer took the initiative of climbing over the back wall and discovered the sliding verandah door was open. He returned for a friend who was staying with him; they entered the bungalow and immediately noticed the near-tropical heat that made the atmosphere intensely cloying. There was five days' mail lying on the mat and the Citroën's ignition keys were on the table, but the lounge was tidy, the kitchen had a few dishes beside the sink and the Newalls' bedroom was averagely untidy. There was nothing suspicious, thought Shearer. But then he was not an intimate of the Newalls.

Maureen Ellam told Philip Falle of the *Jersey Evening Post*, 'I pushed him [her husband] off. I had been so uptight for a couple of days. The storm was here, the roads were impassable and I said, "David, you've bloody got to go over there. Get Mark's phone number and let's find out where they are."'

When David Ellam arrived he saw Maureen's flowers in a vase, and although the wrapper was on the floor he sensed the room was somehow too neat for the Newalls' way of living.

Maureen continued, 'He phoned me as soon as he got there. He'd found Mark's telephone number in Elizabeth's bedroom on the desk. He rang Mark straightaway, got the answerphone and left a message.'

David took up the story. 'I checked the mail. They had two letter boxes, and the one on the front door was never used. It had a bit of plywood over it because anyone looking in could have seen a pile of letters three feet high, so the one in the utility room was used, which you couldn't see through. They also used that as the front door.

'I picked up the mail and I glanced at the dates and put it on the table, turned the central heating down – it was bloody hot in there. I had a quick glance round, phoned Mark up, left a message, then phoned Maureen, said I'd go and sort the roof out first. I remember picking up the dressing-gown which was on the ground, on the slabs near the garden. It was wet, damp – it would be, wouldn't it?

Lying on the ground in October. It had obviously been hung on the whirligig job. It was a turquoisy-coloured housecoat. I think there might have been blood on it, although I didn't realise it at the time. They had obviously washed it. It was away (being forensically examined) for a long time before I was called in by the police to identify it.'

Roderick returned to Jersey on Sunday, 18th October, expressing total mystification, and made a careful search of the bungalow with the Ellams. David noticed stains on the bedroom carpet, but although his wife put them down to spilt tea his suspicions were further aroused when he saw there were no newspapers around. Nicholas had been at his most idiosyncratic over his collection of the papers, religiously picking them up twice a day on his scooter. On Sundays, he would invariably buy a number of the quality broadsheets, but all that David Ellam could see was a couple of Saturday papers in the lounge. Roderick claimed he had taken the Sunday supplements with him to read on the plane, and at the time that seemed an adequate enough explanation. In the mail were unopened birthday cards, letters, circulars and bills.

The Ellams later realised that they had made a considerable mistake by commenting to Roderick on the various 'differences' they saw in the bungalow.

'We did the biggest disservice to the whole of the enquiry that afternoon, unwittingly. We're there, looking for our friends, helping their son, who is concerned about his parents, and we wander round the house and mark his card about everything which appeared wrong. By the time the police got there he'd tidied it all up,' said David Ellam.

Maureen continued: 'I said to the boy, who's my friend's child, he's twenty-three years old, I said, "Right, love, when you've got this lot over come up and food will be ready." "Thank you ever so much, Mrs Ellam, but I really can't. The police are going to come about 7.30 and I promised Mark to have a look at his house for storm damage." I said, "Well, don't go hungry." "I'll grab some fish and chips or something," he said.

'The following morning between 8 and 9 o'clock I phoned him. I said, "All right, love, you awake? Don't you lie in bed all day." "I'm up and about now," he said. "Did you eat yesterday?" He said, "I got some biscuits and one or two bits. I'm all right." "What's the programme today?" I asked. "Well, the police came round yesterday, they might want to see me today and, if he's got to, Mark – he'll come over." I told him we were at the end of the telephone. He said, "OK, talk to you later." That evening, Monday, at 6 o'clock, I rang again. "Have you eaten? Bring your shirts up to be washed . . ." and the boy was . . . agitated. He said, "They're [the police] not interested in where my parents are, they're merely interested in knowing what we were doing." "Well," I said, "that's normal, you know, they're all bloody thick, that's the way they go about it."

'The alarm bells rang in me . . . he was . . . up in the air, just like Elizabeth, and I thought, what has he got to be so uptight about?

'Then Angela Barnes [another friend of the Newalls] made herself acquainted with me, that was on the Sunday night.

'She phoned again on the Monday and said, "What would you say if you knew that boy had slept in his parents' bed last night?" I said, "Why? Did he?" "Yes, he did." I asked her how she knew and she said she'd asked him where he'd slept and he pointed to the bed and said, "There." "Christ," I told her, "I encouraged him to do that."

'When we were looking through the house – the three of us – I picked up the sheets, smelled them, and said that they'd been washed, not ironed, and no one had slept in them either. I'm sure he slept in the bed for that reason.'

Maureen reflected that Roderick must have sensed her disquiet. 'I'm alarmed at the sitting-room. I then walk to her bedroom door and I see in the doorway what looks like a big tea or coffee stain. I am uneasy. I stand at the bedroom door, and I know the bedroom well, and I look at the bedroom. Elizabeth never made a bed until she went to bed, but the bed was made, the duvet was [pulled] up, but it looked wrong, sort of hard.'

David Ellam remembered, 'It didn't flop nicely. It was all stiff.'

Maureen agreed. 'It was as if it had been put on wet. All this time I'm talking, and Roderick's about the place, and I said, "These sheets have been washed, and not ironed. You can smell soap powder. Now when you first sleep in new sheets you can tell, the second night it's not there, your body gets through to it."

'So I'm uneasy about the bedroom, I'm uneasy about the whole thing. I'm feeling everything wrong in that house. But I don't connect the disappearance to the boys then, mind you. Not at all. Somebody has come in and murdered them and taken them away.'

Another couple who were close to Nicholas and Elizabeth were Anne and Robert Blayney who ran a vineyard on the island. Robert remembered that Nicholas, like his son Roderick, was a good sailor and loved the danger. 'Nick loved being stressed sailing and competing with the elements.'

Eight days after the Newalls' disappearance, Anne Blayney came unexpectedly to comfort Roderick and discovered a disturbing and inexplicable atmosphere. As she walked in, she almost tripped over Mark who was unpacking a case in the entrance hall. Anne commented that her sudden appearance made Mark both angry and disconcerted – a fact he made clear by asking her what she was doing there. She told him that she had thought Roderick was on his own and that she had come to look after him. Then she saw Roderick coming out of the sitting-room looking flushed, dishevelled, thoroughly over-heated and over-wrought. Later, with hindsight, Anne Blayney wondered if the brothers thought that she was conducting her own investigation.

'Mark was weird,' she said, 'and behaved as if my presence made him feel uncomfortable.'

Roderick then made her a cup of tea in the kitchen but Anne noticed that his concentration seemed poor. 'I led the conversation and told him we must think things through and find out what was missing in terms of passports, the clothes his parents had been wearing on the night they disappeared, and Elizabeth's handbag.' During this conversation Mark was 'shooting in and out of the kitchen, quite obviously wishing I was not there and anxious to get rid of me.'

Later Roderick went to the Blayneys' home several times to discuss his parents' disappearance and Robert Blayney remembered, 'It was puzzling. Here was an intelligent young man, who had been trained as an army officer, and Anne and I did not think he was making a very good effort at using his brain to try and find out what had happened to Nicholas and Elizabeth. Standing next to the lad I liked a lot, I came to the conclusion that this was an absolute charade he was playing. He must have known all along he was not going to find them. I had a feeling of disbelief and nasty suspicions that they were involved in the disappearance of their parents.'

The Blayneys did not see Roderick again and it is probable that Mark, now the stronger personality, was beginning to control him as he was trying to control everybody else. In an interview with the *Guardian*, Nancy Clarke said, 'Mark seemed to be the person who was in control. He made any statements that needed to be made to the police, but Mark is always in control. He has control over Roderick, he even seems to have control over the police and the legal profession.' Maureen Ellam added that Elizabeth was indulgent of Roderick's naughty, arrogant charm but she, Maureen, found Mark difficult. 'I couldn't abide the boy. He was so assured. "That awful boy" was how he was referred to by all four of us – Nick, Liz and us. There was something about him which just set your teeth on edge.' Rather more perceptively, Nicholas Newall's twin brother Stephen said, 'We watched from the sidelines and saw two very badly treated little boys.' He added that Mark was the son who 'always came in for the heavy end of things.'

But Mark, already a formidable figure, was very much 'in control' and would remain so for a long time to come.

The case was initially viewed as a missing persons investigation, but on 20th October an incident room was set up and Dr David Northcott, a Home Office scientist from the Aldermaston Forensic Centre, arrived to make a more detailed examination. What he discovered basically changed the missing persons investigation into a murder enquiry, but because the police suspected that Roderick and Mark were in some way involved in their parents' disappearance, the decision was taken to keep the information secret. Nobody was told, including the Ellams. On this basis, it was felt, they could trap any suspects more easily.

Detective Inspector Jim Adamson later told Channel TV after he and Detective Inspector Graham Nimmo had visited the brothers at their parents' home, 'They didn't appear to be over-concerned, as I would be if my parents had gone missing. They were very cool and calm about it, and very evasive. I wrote in my notebook that I didn't believe a word that they had said.'

Nimmo remembered: 'We went with an open mind. Roderick had been drinking. Mark hadn't and was the calmer of the two. Mark got very concerned about Roderick's attitude and even shouted at him to stop being so silly and to get out of the room.'

It was Nimmo who first spotted blood on the poker. 'They were two of the most arrogant supercilious young men that I have ever met in twenty-five years. I still have difficulty comprehending what happened and how they did it but I believe they were brought up to do that. That may sound strange. They hated their parents. I couldn't put my finger on when they started to hate them but it was very obvious from the beginning.'

Dr Northcott spent four days at the bungalow, discovering two areas in the house that were blood-stained. He found a large number of very small blood specks around the fireplace in the lounge and also in the main bedroom, just inside the door. Both these areas had been cleaned but a large number of the spots were found on dark surfaces that had been overlooked during the clean-up operation. Northcott also discovered green and white fibres which indicated that J-cloths had been used which were identical to a box in the kitchen. On 16th November 1987, Professor Cameron, the Home Office Pathologist from London Medical College, arrived on Jersey to help assess Mr Northcott's findings. They both concluded that violent assaults had taken place in the two areas of the bungalow where the blood had been discovered. Blood spots were also found on a poker in the lounge and on a pair of jeans in the spare bedroom. The hired van was impounded by the police and close examination revealed minute specks of blood in the rear. The blood in the lounge was discovered to be the same group as Nicholas's twin brother Stephen. In the bedroom, the blood was found to be in the same group as Elizabeth's.

The inadequate attempts to clean up the two rooms clearly showed great and panicky haste. The carpets and walls had either been washed or scrubbed, the heating had been turned up to dry out the bungalow and a duvet in the bedroom had probably been hurriedly washed and put back on the bed in a damp condition. Also, some books and a rug from the lounge appeared to be missing.

The clothes that the Newalls had been wearing at the dinner with their sons were also missing, although Mark claimed that they were wearing casual outfits when he last saw them at home.

As a result of all this evidence, the Jersey police assumed that Nicholas and Elizabeth Newall were murdered between 11th and 17th October 1987.

Roderick and Mark Newall were first interviewed by the police on 20th October and gave reasonably comprehensive statements. The policy of sitting it out indefinitely was the only action Roderick Newall could take. He must have realised he was a prime suspect but he used his authority to assure the Ellams and the police that he was every bit as concerned as they were. Neither of the brothers provided an explanation but Mark, the cooler and more level-headed of the two, gave interviews to the press that were designed to be as subtle as possible. He expressed concern, gravity and frankness as is epitomised in the Newsfile section of the *Jersey Evening Post* on Monday,

2nd November 1987, three weeks after the disappearance of Nicholas and Elizabeth.

The chances of them being alive are very slim
Three weeks after his parents vanished without trace from their bungalow at Clos de l'Atlantique, St Brelade, 21-year-old Mark Newall is trying desperately to find some rational or logical explanation for their disappearance.

Over and over again he has gone through the theories which detectives – amateur and professional, for the disappearance of Nicholas and Elizabeth Newall has provoked an enormous amount of public discussion – have looked at.

'If you look at the available facts in a logical way, they do not fit any of the theories of an accident, kidnap, suicide or murder, and therefore the odds are that something illogical has happened to them,' he said.

'Either way it just does not make any sense.'

Mark is a stockbroker working for Sheppard's whose offices are on the Esplanade, St Helier, but in recent times he has been based at the firm's London office, working in Jersey only rarely.

He and his brother Roderick, a 22-year-old Lieutenant with the Royal Green Jackets in Winchester, flew to Jersey on the evening of Friday, October 9th, partly to attend a family dinner the following night in advance of their mother's 48th birthday the following week.

Mark had recently bought a house, La Falaise, at Noirmont and wanted to move some possessions into there over the weekend, and on Saturday he and his father drove to pick up the Falles van hired for the purpose.

When he and Roderick arrived at their parents' home

Nicholas Newall

Elizabeth Newall

Roderick Newall at St Michael's School, Jersey, aged about six.

Mark Newall at the same school.

Mark Newall, January 1991.

Roderick Newall in St Helier, Jersey, April / May 1988, after being bailed on a drugs charge for which he was later gaoled for one month.

Mark Newall with his father's twin, Stephen, and Aunt Gaye after the funeral of their great-uncle Kenneth Newall, who died in Sark a few weeks after the murders.

Roderick (right) and Mark leave the church after Kenneth Newall's funeral, 1988.

Maureen and David Ellam, who bought Crow's Nest from the Newalls.
Mrs Ellam has been described as 'something of a Miss Marple'.

Crow's Nest, the luxury house at Greve-de-Lecq, Jersey, the former
home of the Newalls, near which the bodies were buried.

The Newall's bungalow at Clos de L'Atlantique, St Brelade, Jersey. It was at the door on the left that Roderick met Maureen Ellam on the morning after the murders.

The bedroom and sitting room of the Newalls' home.

The Sea Crest Hotel and Restaurant, where Elizabeth and Nicholas Newall were last seen alive.

Detective Inspector Martin Fitzgerald at a Press Conference in July, 1994, with rice flail and axe.

The search at the scene of the fire at Greve-de-Lecq, where evidence of the frantic 'clean-up' operation was found.

Roderick directs the police to where his parents' bodies were buried,
November, 1993.

that Saturday evening, a pre-dinner bottle of Champagne was being cooled.

Mark explained that he drinks very rarely – and only vodka when he does.

'They had the Champagne before we left for the Sea Crest, and I drove, both there and back,' he said.

Although the police have issued descriptions of what his parents are thought to have been wearing at dinner, Mark is not at all certain about their clothing – either then or when he and Roderick left the property the following afternoon.

'Others are a lot surer about their clothing than I am, but at the time we left the house on Sunday they were certainly wearing casual clothes – I know what sort of clothing they would have been wearing, but I can't be certain exactly what they were wearing,' he said.

The family left the Sea Crest at about midnight, and Mark recalls that the others had more to drink when they returned to Clos de l'Atlantique.

'They had an 18-year-old single malt whisky, the Macallan, at the house when we returned,' he said.

Although he cannot be certain when he and Roderick left their parents' home – they were eating there but sleeping at Mark's house at Noirmont – he thinks that it was about 2.30 or 3 a.m. on the Sunday.

They returned relatively early the following morning, about 8.30 a.m., and were there when Mrs Maureen Ellam arrived with a bouquet of flowers a few minutes after nine.

Mark Newall is not certain that the description of the clothes thought to be missing from the house is restricted to those his parents were wearing at the Saturday night dinner.

'I believe that there is more than one outfit missing

from my mother's wardrobe, and no one knows my father's wardrobe well enough to know which, if any, of his casual clothes are missing,' he said.

When he and his brother left for the airport that Sunday afternoon, their parents remained at home enjoying a quiet and typical Sunday.

'I dropped Roderick off at the airport, then returned to my house to pick up some baggage before going to the airport myself,' he said.

Mark's flight was later than his brother's, and he left his car, a Toyota MR2 sports model, at the airport.

'I could not get out on the ferry that day, and so I returned to Jersey late on the following Tuesday to pick it up, along with the remainder of my clothes which I had left at my own house,' he said.

Mark arrived back on the island shortly after 8 p.m. on that Tuesday.

He picked up his car from the airport car park, drove to his house at Noirmont, picked up his clothes from there, his ferry ticket from his firm's offices on the Esplanade, and checked in at the British Channel Islands Ferries terminal less than an hour after his aircraft touched down.

Asked if his parents had any enemies, or if there had been anything unpleasant in connection with any of their business arrangements, particularly in Spain, Mark said: 'I know very little about Spain and their life there, but had there been any problem I would have been the first to know, particularly if there was a financial problem or anything of that sort.'

For two of the last three weeks Mark and other members of the family have been in close contact with senior police officers who are investigating his parents' disappearance.

What, then, does he think has happened to his parents, and while obviously hoping that they are still alive, where does he think they are?

'If we are to look at it realistically, then the chances of them being alive are very slim,' he said.

'People don't just disappear, and then walk through the door three weeks later and say "Hi, folks."'

Obviously Mark must have had a very hard job to keep cool. The pressure on both brothers was increasing daily and Mark must have thought there was every possibility Roderick would crack. The disappearance was the talk of the island and the Ellams, in co-operation with Philip Falle of the *Jersey Evening Post*, were pressing hard. Apart from being a senior reporter Falle had previously been a police officer and his experience told him that the disappearance of Nicholas and Elizabeth Newall was a deeply suspicious event and that, in some way, their two sons were involved. So Falle ran the following piece in the *Jersey Evening Post* as the beginning of a gathering campaign to ventilate the circumstances – as well as to put pressure on the Newall brothers.

Close friends admit couple's disappearance is baffling
David and Maureen Ellam speak of Nicholas and Elizabeth as if they have known them all their lives.

They know what the Newalls liked to eat and drink, how they dressed, what they enjoyed doing, and even how they may have reacted to certain situations.

What they don't know is where they are, and Maureen Ellam in particular admits that the strain is getting her down.

'Like everyone else we want them found, whatever has happened to them,' she said.

'We want an end to this uncertainty because we just can't cope with it any more, and if it is getting to us like this, what must it be like for the family?'

The couples met only last year, when the Ellams first visited what is now their home, the appropriately named Crow's Nest, which then belonged to Nicholas and Elizabeth Newall.

Perched high above the Prince of Wales Hotel on the St Ouen side of Greve de Lecq, Crow's Nest has what must be one of the island's most panoramic views.

In the year since they bought the property, David and Maureen Ellam have in their own words, 'worked and worked' on the house, with the interest and encouragement of the previous owners.

'The whole time we've been working on it both Nicholas and Elizabeth have known exactly what we wanted to do – exactly what we've been trying to achieve, and each time they returned to Jersey from Spain they would come round as soon as they could to see the progress which had been made,' said Mrs Ellam.

They are as baffled as the police and the Newall family about the couple's disappearance, and are adamant that it is as improbable as it can be that they have merely gone away without telling anyone.

'Elizabeth is a great one for keeping in contact,' said Mrs Ellam. 'I have known them give us a date on which they expected to return to Spain, and then she would write saying that it would not be that day but a few days earlier or later.

'She is a compulsive telephoner and would ring about anything, or call round, as they did on that Saturday morning [10th October].'

Maureen Ellam recalled her visit to the Newalls' home

at Clos de l'Atlantique on the morning of Sunday, 11 October.

'Roderick did not recognise me at first – we had only met on one occasion, and that was when David and I first went round to view Crow's Nest – so I hurriedly introduced myself as I gave him the flowers,' she said.

'I told him that I could not stay but explained that the flowers were for Elizabeth, and when he said that she and Nicholas were still asleep, made some flippant remark before I left.'

As soon as she arrived home after collecting her brother from the airport, Mrs Ellam asked her husband if Elizabeth had rung.

'I was surprised when he said she had not, because I had it in my mind that she would have phoned. It would have been the first thing she would have done, and I still cannot understand why she didn't.'

That Sunday passed, as did the first few days of the following week, with both the Ellams becoming more and more anxious.

'We telephoned, but there was always no reply, but we became really concerned after the storm on the Friday – after Nicholas and Elizabeth had failed to keep a date with us.'

Eventually Maureen Ellam contacted the States police for advice, and David Ellam went to the Newalls' home.

'As a result of that I finally made contact with Roderick, and met him at the airport when he came over on the following Sunday. We drove down to the police together to report Nicholas and Elizabeth missing,' she said.

'We are as mystified now as we were then. We just want them found, because I don't think I can cope with the strain for very much longer.

'I hope and pray that they are alive, and that there is some simple explanation for all this, but I can't honestly see one.

'Either way, whatever has happened we want them found.'

Both David and Maureen Ellam confirm the generally accepted view that the Newalls were a very close and loving couple.

'They lived for each other, did everything together, and were very, very happy.'

Philip Falle remembered that he put to Mark in his original interview with him in October 1987 that people were suggesting he and Roderick knew more about their parents' disappearance than they had told the police. The exact wording was as follows, but it was not published at the time as it was well before anything was known about the Newall brothers' involvement in their parents' disappearance.

'Do you realise what people are saying about this?'

Mark Newall replied, 'No. What?'

'They are saying you and your brother know more about this than you had told the police.'

There was no response.

'Well – what do you say to that?'

Mark replied, 'I wouldn't deign to answer such a question, no matter who asked it.'

The interview had been arranged in a hotel lounge and although it appeared unproductive Falle noticed two important factors. Firstly, during the discussion, Mark continually held his car keys tightly in a closed fist until his knuckles were white and he must have been in considerable pain. Did this aid his powers of concentration and his determination not to give his brother away? Also, considering a reporter had just made a very sinister implication,

Mark did not walk out – or refer the matter to the police, which increased Falle's suspicions that there was something very wrong.

Meanwhile, an intensive search of the island was begun which initially involved hundreds of police officers. The area around the bungalow in Clos de l'Atlantique, known as Las Pulente, was carefully scrutinised but nothing was found. Gradually the search was widened to surrounding areas including those to the east of Greve de Lecq and the refuse dump at La Saline. Dogs capable of detecting buried corpses were brought in from England, as were radar devices, heat-seeking equipment and helicopters, but no amount of sophisticated equipment could find the shallow grave where Nicholas and Elizabeth lay in the field a few hundred yards from their former home.

Slowly the investigation bore fruit with the discovery of the spade and the remains of the fire. Maureen Ellam later recalled that she had seen Roderick Newall, looking 'angry and red-faced', hurrying past her home which was close to the site of the fire. She asked him what he had been doing but he merely replied that he had been walking on the headland.

Greve de Lecq was searched, but no evidence of any bodies was discovered.

Meanwhile, an increasing number of people on Jersey began to suspect the Newall brothers were involved in their parents' disappearance, but there seemed to be frustratingly little evidence. As yet, the full details of Uncle Sark's bequest had not been made public and Mark, originally cool, confident, even arrogant in his dealings with the press, was possibly keeping a low public profile after his harrowing interview in the hotel.

Roderick, however, was now becoming oppressed by guilt, continuously mentally reliving the events and beginning to waver. The institutionalism of the Royal Green Jackets which he dare not leave too early must have been something of a comfort to him, however much he hated the army. Nothing changed, routine continued and he knew that far away in Jersey the police were at an impasse, forced to play a waiting game, no doubt hoping that he would crack – or that some evidence would come to light that would not only incriminate the Newall brothers but would also stand up in court.

On Jersey, speculation and rumour were rife, but little of it was of any use to the police. Apart from the Ellams, Nicholas and Elizabeth Newall only had a few close friends and, because they spent so many months of the year at their villa in Spain, were not seen as permanent Jersey residents. This elusiveness seemed to be another reason why the enquiry, still officially in its 'missing persons' mode, remained unproductive.

It was therefore decided to widen the investigation as the police wondered whether there might be some kind of Spanish connection. Local residents claimed that a distinctive car – a pink Mercedes with a foreign number plate and left-hand drive – had been seen outside the Newall home at 9 Clos de l'Atlantique on a number of occasions and had often been parked there for at least two hours at a time. The *Jersey Evening Post* reported on 29th October, 'Confirmation that such a car had been driven on island roads has come from several police officers who recall seeing it, but as yet there are no clues to its occupants, although detectives have not ruled out the possibility that it could have been friends of the couple from Spain.'

Nicholas and Elizabeth had been due to return to Spain on 20th October, and had booked a passage on the *Solidor* to St Malo. In the back bedroom of the bungalow were a number of packing cases containing such unrevealing items as salad shakers and cleaning materials. The police also visited the Newalls' Spanish villa near Alicante, but once again nothing of significance was discovered.

In Spain, reactions were shock, disbelief and puzzlement. Mrs Adeline Glyn-Evans said she was hoping it was kidnapping and nothing worse. 'Friends all around here are absolutely shattered. We just can't believe it. They're not the sort of people to do anything silly. If anything, it's kidnapping – least, that's what we hope, and nothing worse.' Asked by a reporter if she thought the Newalls might have committed suicide, Mrs Glyn-Evans replied hotly, 'Good grief, no. They are just not the sort of people. They're a terribly happy pair, full of fun and life.'

No one in Spain could throw any light on the mysterious pink Mercedes but the car initiated further red herrings. Why, asked the police, did the Newalls always drive to Javea in their locally registered Renault when they had a small Fiat Panda garaged at the villa? This was probably only yet another example of Nicholas's frugality, for it would be far cheaper to drive the Renault to Spain than pay expensive airfares, and to use the Fiat Panda, with its smaller petrol consumption, when they arrived. This was the sort of saving that Nicholas Newall had always been obsessed with.

The then head of Jersey's CID, Detective Chief Inspector Martyn Le Brocq, made this statement:

'We are following up every piece of information we get, no matter how small or insignificant it might appear to the informant, but we are desperate for anyone who has either seen or spoken to the couple since 6th October –

and in particular those who have made contact since the weekend of the 10th and 11th – to come forward. At the moment we have a full incident room in operation. We have as many as sixty officers working on the case. We intend to make further searches using the French helicopter from the French rescue service CROSSMA and we are not even sure we are investigating a crime. Their continued disappearance is as baffling for us as it is distressing for the family, and that is why I appeal to anyone who has any information at all to come forward.'

There was more than a hint of defensiveness in this statement, but the police were still keeping the forensic evidence in the background. While they re-interviewed Roderick and Mark, the rumours of a Spanish connection served as a necessary distraction for a public that wanted action. So did the Ellams, who were still pushing as hard as they could for an answer to their close friends' disappearance. Throughout the enquiry the Ellams were persistent and a force to be reckoned with, as were other friends of the Newalls including Angela Barnes and vineyard owners Bob and Anne Blayney.

Another red herring was the discovery that Nicholas and Elizabeth Newall had two passports. The local passport office confirmed that the Newalls had reported their passports stolen in December 1984 and had been issued with new ones. Two passports had already been found at the bungalow and it had previously been thought that they could not have travelled outside the Channel Islands or the UK, but the existence of another two which were not at the bungalow opened up the possibility that they could be abroad.

Perhaps to Roderick Newall's relief, the Spanish connection began not only to gather momentum but to gradually grow a myth of its own. The Jersey police visited Spain and decided that the two sets of passports were probably used to avoid paying Spanish tax. After a five-day investigation, the police concluded Nicholas and Elizabeth Newall apparently obtained the extra set by falsely claiming their passports had been stolen in December 1984. They were then issued with new ones. If the Newalls were resident in Spain for over ninety consecutive days, they would be liable to pay tax, and the police believed that they may have obtained two sets to demonstrate that they were not residents when they entered and left the country. They also discovered that the Newall parents had many bank accounts in a number of countries, including Spain, the UK and possibly Switzerland. This is hardly surprising, however, as all their financial affairs were managed by Mark, who naturally wanted to ensure they made as much money as possible; Nicholas would certainly have been enthusiastic about that.

After searching the couple's villa, which had recently been extended to include a self-contained flat, they found a large number of documents and statements revealing the wide extent of their financial affairs. Nicholas owned a mini home computer on which he kept a meticulous record of details of their life and over twenty police officers began to examine between forty and fifty computer discs for any further clues as to their disappearance.

One of the most puzzling features to emerge from the officers' visit to Spain were the many faces of Mr Newall. He wore spectacles and was clean-shaven in Jersey, but had a beard and no glasses in Spain. Probably Nicholas regarded the Mediterranean life as one in which he could unwind and was not obliged to 'keep up appearances' as he may have wished to do in Jersey. But because of their abrupt disappearance, the fact that Nicholas and Elizabeth had been wiped clean away from their home, more sinister links, including abduction by the Mafia, were being hinted at.

After interviewing all the couple's friends and acquaintances in Spain, where they spent about ten months of every year, the police discovered Nicholas had a pilot's licence and a Spanish-registered car. Once again this fuelled popular imagination, painting a possible portrait of Nicholas Newall being some kind of international racketeer. The British press had already elevated his status to near-millionaire and speculation about drug deals abroad and crooked contacts abounded. How seriously the police really took all this it is difficult to say, but although they were clearly duty bound to investigate Nicholas and Elizabeth's Spanish life, they may well have also been extending their waiting game with Roderick and Mark. On 5th November the *Jersey Evening Post* reported:

'From all the background information gained in Spain, police now wish to interview more of the couple's friends and associates in the UK, and they will also be re-interviewing the Newalls' two sons Roderick and Mark.

'Following their investigations, police now have more details of the couple's background, but say they are still no closer to solving the mystery. So far absolutely nothing has shed any light on the couple's whereabouts.

'"We have been given no indication whatsoever of whether they are alive or whether they are dead," said Inspector Nimo.'

The Spanish connection petered out completely when the missing set of passports was found after a more intensive search at the bungalow, and the activity on the case reached an all-time low. As the report of Mafia links died down, another strange episode followed when the Jersey police allowed a psychic investigator to intervene. Once again, however, this was probably another attempt to keep the story alive – and therefore to continue the pressure on the Newall brothers.

Brian Terriss, an allegedly psychic Guernsey doctor, believed that Nicholas and Elizabeth were dead, but he volunteered his services to establish the whereabouts of the bodies. Psychics do sometimes help with detection, the police taking the view that it is better for the psychic to be under their control than wandering about the countryside pursued by a posse of reporters.

Terriss, who had already reputedly discovered the dead body of a Guernsey resident, Lorraine Vaudin, in August, thought that Nicholas Newall's body was on the cliffs above Portelet and that Elizabeth's had drifted out to sea. Terriss's technique was to use his powers in conjunction with maps, compasses, magnets and personal possessions. He gave the press this statement, whilst waiting for the Newall family to agree to hand over the necessary items: 'I saw a picture of the missing couple in a national newspaper and used that. As regards the man, I think he is still on the cliffs, but dead as well. She went first and tumbled into the water. He took the nearest way down, slipped and fell down the cliffs. I have [psychically] tried Spain, but there is no location of the couple in that country. I reckon they are both dead. I might be wrong. I am not perfect.'

He was certainly a little off target on the evidence; Terriss also claimed that the Newalls were half-way through a meal when they 'felt they had had enough' and decided to go out for a walk. 'From my observations,' he continued, 'I think there is somebody else – a friend, a woman. She probably offered them a lift, stopped somewhere near the cliffs, and let them out to walk there.' He added that he might go to Jersey and 'have a go myself, but I'm not a climber.'

Eventually, with the Newalls now missing for three weeks, the family loaned Terriss some of Nicholas and Elizabeth's possessions and he began his own intuitive investigation.

Meanwhile, two local officers from the Jersey police appeared on BBC TV's *Crimewatch UK* to enlist the help of viewers to solve the mystery of the Newalls' disappearance – a mystery that was now being compared to that of the *Marie Celeste*, the ship that was found afloat, with half-eaten meals and signs of recent occupation, but whose officers and crew were never seen again.

Although a few sightings were made by BBC viewers, they turned out to be of a couple touring the island who had a vague resemblance to the Newalls. Enquiries by Jersey officers, Detective Inspectors Graham Nimmo and Detective James Adamson, spread from the island to London, Kent, Edinburgh and Glasgow, but every lead dried up and Terriss, although not officially called to the island by the police, stated that the objects given to him – a pipe, a lipstick and scarves – had not provided any more psychic information beyond what he had gained from the cuttings.

Later Terriss explained, 'A blood-hound picks a scent up, but he gets to a point where he gets confused. That's what's happened to me. I must have gone over with the wrong thoughts.' So the psychic blood-hound was as stymied as the police. But maybe they should have given him Roderick Newall's old school ties; perhaps that would have done the trick.

4

On 21st November 1987, the family's benefactor, Kenneth Newall, died; his funeral was held in Guernsey on Wednesday, 25th November. Detective Inspector Nimmo was despatched there to be available to any relative or friend who wanted to confide in him. Amongst the mourners were Mark and Roderick Newall. Once again carefully fronting the situation, Mark told the *Jersey Evening Post* that he was planning to return to Jersey from London in the near future. The Newalls had now vanished for over six weeks and Mark said that he had also visited Spain. When asked what thoughts he and his brother had had about their missing parents, he declined to comment. On 27th November 1987, Roderick and Mark were interviewed at length by Detective Inspector Nimmo and the interviews, each taking several hours, were tape recorded. Both the brothers stated, as they had done previously, that their parents were alive and well on the afternoon of Sunday 11th October 1987 when they had left them at their home at Clos de l'Atlantique to return to England.

Accompanied by DI Adamson, DI Nimmo spoke to relations and friends at the funeral. Stephen, Nicholas's twin brother, was there but there were no fresh leads. The next day Mark went to police headquarters in Jersey to 'find out if there were any further developments in the enquiry'. No doubt he was questioned with his lawyer present yet again, but his defensive skills were growing. Now his brother was once again back in the safe haven of the army, Mark was having to shoulder increasing pressure, but this he was well able to cope with. To have convinced his father that he could successfully handle his financial affairs at such a young age was an achievement in itself and must have greatly bolstered Mark's confidence.

The Newalls' attitude to police officers on the case bordered on arrogance. Indeed, the police concerned in the initial investigation may well have found themselves feeling inferior to both brothers and that is probably why the two principal officers placed in charge of the later stages of the case were specifically chosen to avoid such a situation developing. Assistant Chief Officer, Paul Marks, was the son of a schoolmaster and had been taught by his own father at prep school, whilst Detective Sergeant Charlie MacDowall had been to a boarding school.

Meanwhile, rumours continued to spread. In one speculation, Nicholas was reputed to have been involved in a drug-running operation between Spain and America; he and Elizabeth were said to have been killed by a Mafia hit-man, and their bodies either buried at sea or incinerated. Alternatively, the speculators imagined the couple might have made a deliberate disappearance in the style of Lord Lucan.

On Wednesday, 23rd December, the police accepted that the Newalls were probably dead. They had been missing for ten weeks, and although the forensic results had still not been publicly revealed, there was little doubt they had been murdered. Now heading the investigation, DI Nimmo firmly stated that ten officers would still remain on the case until the matter was resolved. Routine enquiries, he added, were being made into the Newalls' financial affairs in Switzerland and America, but this did not imply their dealings were in any way irregular. The *Jersey Evening Post* of the same date added, 'The couple's younger son, Mark, a 21-year-old stockbroker in London, could not be contacted this morning. He is believed to be on holiday in Spain.'

On 5th January 1988, Mark told the *Jersey Evening Post* from London that 'neither he nor any member of his family had any comment to make at the moment, and were leaving it to the police.' Later in January, the Newalls' back garden was searched, using a scientist and sub-surface radar equipment from the UK, at a cost of £4,500. Accompanying the scientist, whose name was not revealed, were representatives of the Scientific Research and Development Branch of the Home Office who were currently studying this kind of sub-surface radar system and wanted the chance to test it out in the Newalls' back garden. Apparently the technique had only been developed within the last six months and held considerable implications for investigations in the future.

The police claimed that they wanted to eliminate the Newalls' garden from their enquiries which apparently could not have been done before, short of digging it up completely. Despite this explanation, it does seem strange that the Jersey police did not undertake such a dig much earlier, particularly as they had so many officers on the case at the beginning of their enquiries.

Superintendent Bob Le Breton explained how the radar equipment functioned: 'A return signal is analysed, digitised and processed into a computer, which produces a video image. It will produce a signal of everything which is in the subsoil. If we find nothing in the garden, we will be looking at searching other areas.'

'Searching other areas' with this sophisticated and highly sensitive equipment must have been the phrase that really alarmed Roderick Newall; there can be little doubt that he must have wondered if the police were slowly homing in on that lonely grave in the field near the sea.

Mark, too, must have found the pressure very difficult, particularly as he was surely all too well aware of the almost inevitable suspicion on the part of the police that it was a pre-planned murder. How he must have wished he had been able to persuade his brother to give himself up on that terrible night of 10th October. As a result Roderick might have received a manslaughter charge, but only if he had pleaded not guilty to murder. It would, however, always have been difficult to explain away two deaths. How serious had Roderick been in threatening to take his own life? Perhaps Mark was beginning to wonder if this had been merely histrionics, or could Roderick have been hoping that he might get away with the crime and inherit Uncle Sark's money? Either way, there is no doubt that Roderick was likely to be the first to crack.

5

In the spring of 1988 Roderick resigned his commission with the Royal Green Jackets and left the army. The hunt for his parents' bodies was escalating with revelations at last from the police that they had found bloodstains in the house. Public pressure had by now become so intense that they obviously felt they could no longer withhold the information. Roderick, either because he wanted to watch over his parents' graves again or because he had things to pick up, returned to the island.

Foolishly, he brought cannabis with him, needing a relaxant and no doubt terrified of getting drunk and letting something slip. Jersey takes a punitive view on drugs and even first offenders are often jailed for a week or so. Roderick, however, was seen to be importing drugs and therefore this was a more serious charge.

As Roderick arrived from Southampton on 29th February 1988, Jersey's new sniffer dogs were in operation and passengers were asked to wait in a lounge. A positive indication was made when a dog was in Roderick Newall's vicinity and he was searched. In his briefcase three small pieces of resin and a set of scales were discovered. The total amount was 80 mg but more was later discovered at

La Falaise, Rue de Noirmont (Mark's house), which was where Roderick told Customs he had stayed on previous visits to the island. Obviously Nicholas and Elizabeth's bungalow was now police-sealed.

Roderick told Customs officers that additional cannabis resin discovered at his brother's house was for personal use and that he had smoked the drug because of his 'unhappy bereavement'. He appeared in the police court on 11th March, and the case was adjourned for three weeks. His bail was set at £250 and Roderick was ordered to stay on the island, surrender his passport and make twice-weekly visits to police headquarters.

His defence counsel stated that everyone was aware of the unfortunate circumstances surrounding the family and added that his client wanted to leave the island soon to 'sort out some family matters abroad'. The magistrate however refused to comply with this or to speed up the probation officer's interview, saying it would be wrong to show favouritism. He added that it was an extremely serious offence, particularly in 'view of the fact that Newall was a retired army officer and should have been setting a good example'.

As Roderick had now trapped himself on the island he was all too well aware that the search, although revealing nothing new at Clos de l'Atlantique, was going to be extended and that the highly sophisticated radar device was still going to be used.

At a later hearing, Roderick's defence counsel, Advocate David Le Quesne, proposed that Newall should leave the island and live with his uncle in Scotland, still reporting to local police each day with his passport withdrawn, but someone informed on him and he was arrested again for smoking cannabis while on bail. This latest breach forestalled Le Quesne's plea which 'would prevent Newall languishing on Jersey, living alone in his brother's house, dwelling on the family tragedy, his parents now being presumed dead and in an atmosphere where he was under pressure from media and public interest and subjected to constant police attention for various reasons'.

Having listened to the defence's submission, Magistrate Tom Dorey eventually decided that Roderick should be remanded in custody while further enquiries were made, especially as he had committed a second offence while on bail. The *Jersey Evening Post* reported, 'He [Mr Dorey] was satisfied that knowing a prison sentence might be imposed Newall would be tempted to abscond, but the most important consideration was his "blatant disregard" for the law in re-offending while on bail, he said.'

Officially, a police spokesman stated that they did 'not wish to talk to Newall further in relation to the drugs charges and that the enquiries referred to in court were being made by the army's special investigation branch'.

However, it must be stressed that it is highly unlikely there was any sharing of information between police and Customs officers – there rarely is – and the fact that the man arrested for importing cannabis was Roderick Newall came as a surprise. Possibly, however, the police were hoping he would finally confess in prison, particularly when he heard that the Ellams had sent out a plea to the general public to search for the missing couple over the Bank Holiday weekend. Those who suspected Roderick and Mark were involved in the disappearance of their parents were increasing in number and it was a common topic of conversation on the island as to 'where the boys had put them'.

In making their plea, the Ellams stated that their 'main concern in making a public appeal for help to find their friends, who they now accepted must have been murdered, was to lay them to rest in the decent manner which society demands'. There was a good deal of response but, once again, nothing came of it.

By now Roderick must have been aware, not only of the Ellams' and other people's suspicions about his and Mark's involvement in their parents' disappearance, but that their friends' persistence was not going to waver. Also, although in prison on remand, Roderick would have been allowed newspapers so he would have been alarmed to read the news of his own custody in the same reports as the continued investigation. The police – and press – were hoping the general public would put two and two together. Certainly Roderick did – and immediately went on a hunger strike.

Roderick Newall's strike lasted four days and the governor of La Moye prison, Keith Wheeler, confirmed this to the *Jersey Evening Post* on 5th April. 'He is thought to be protesting about the refusal of his bail application.'

On 6th April 1988, Roderick Newall ended his strike just as the head of the Suffolk CID, Detective Chief Superintendent John Saunders, was called in to 'review the progress of the investigation'. The Jersey police emphasised that Saunders would not be carrying out his own research but that 'his job would be to bring a fresh and experienced outlook to the enquiry, and to act in an advisory capacity'. In other words the Jersey police had reached a total impasse, the investigation had ground to a halt and a fresh approach was urgently needed. Ironically, with the prime suspect incarcerated in La Moye prison on other charges, a result was so near – yet so far.

Police sniffer dogs had recently been brought in from England and had discovered items of clothing on the north coast that might possibly belong to Nicholas and Elizabeth Newall. This slender find at least produced some movement in an enquiry that seemed to have run out of steam, but a spokesman stated the police were 'still awaiting the forensic examination'. Somehow the pot had to be kept boiling, but could the experienced and objective Saunders work a miracle?

6

In an interview with Philip Falle on 30th April 1988, Detective Chief Superintendent John Saunders told him, 'I think their disappearance occurred before the storm, and I don't think it hampered enquiries as such, although it may still be assisting in the concealment of bodies.

'On that score, the police themselves have searched a lot of areas as a result of both their own initiative, and as a result of the public suggesting that they search particular areas.

'But there's still a lot that the public could well be able to do, particularly over the forthcoming Bank Holidays, in going out for themselves and seeing if they can find anything suspicious . . .

'What I do want to stress is that the review has not uncovered inefficiency, inadequacy or incompetence. It's uncovered new theories on which to work, but you would expect that from a fresh eye.

'There's a tremendous benefit in getting someone in from the outside, and it's important as well, from my point of view, that you come with an open mind and look at all possibilities.

'I have been totally open-minded throughout, and

you've got to consider every conceivable theory and possibility, and that's what I've done . . .

'It's a difficult enquiry to resolve. I don't think there is any such thing as a perfect murder, because whoever commits an offence of this nature must realise that they take on a tremendous amount of expertise, apart from it being a challenge for the police,' he said.

'People who commit murder can very often make things extremely difficult for those enquiring into them, but police officers on their own don't solve murders; the public very often assist in solving them, very often with the brilliant work of scientists and technologists, and I'm quite certain that in this case it will be a combination of the three.'

Asked about the items which were found on the north coast while specialist police dogs from the Lancashire police were on the island, Saunders said that the results of tests on those items were still being awaited.

'Again, people must not see that as a sign of weakness or read anything into the delay. Unfortunately, all matters, serious though this one is, have to be dealt with according to an order of priorities with the scientists, and eventually we shall get the results,' he said.

'It may well take a long time but time-scales must be seen as unimportant – it's the end result that counts . . .

'It's important that this case must be kept alive through the media, because I am convinced that the public can still help the police.

'People who have already been seen by the police and who have made statements must sit down again and examine in their minds what they told us previously.

'They must think about that extra detail which could help – it may seem insignificant but it could be vital and the general public must also be vigilant when they are out and about, and contact the police about anything suspicious . . .'

Roderick was released from La Moye prison in April 1988 and travelled to Spain where the family yacht, the *Chanson du Lecq*, was based. For some weeks he sailed around the Mediterranean. He was a highly competent yachtsman but the sea must have given him little comfort for he was still prey to increasing guilt. To block this out he knew that he would eventually have to sail as far away from Jersey as he could. The South Atlantic and the Falklands seemed an appropriate wilderness.

Meanwhile, back on the island, the friends of Nicholas and Elizabeth must have been all too well aware that the bird had flown.

Saunders' advice, however, prompted a flurry of activity as, on 17th May 1988, more forensic tests were carried out on the still-sealed bungalow. At the same time, the police announced that this revised investigation was going to take several months and during the next few weeks there would be more house-to-house enquiries in St Brelade – the area around the Newalls' home – and several sections of land not previously searched would be closely examined. In addition to this they announced that 'a substantial number of people will be interviewed, both in Jersey and the UK.' The police added that this included some of those who had been interviewed already; Nicholas's twin brother and his wife in Scotland, as well as Mark Newall, were included in the list.

The weeks dragged by with little revelation, but on 29th June the *Jersey Evening Post* hopefully reported, 'The potential murder case involving the missing St Brelade couple, Nicholas and Elizabeth Newall, may soon reach what the police describe as a satisfactory conclusion, but they are not prepared to say when or even if any arrests will be made.' Clearly bets were being hedged, for the waiting game could prove to be a long one.

The officer currently in charge of the investigation said that he was 'cautiously optimistic that there may be some light at the end of the tunnel'. However, the appeals for information from the general public about the tools and other items that had been bought from Norman Ltd for £103.42 on the day the Newalls were last seen alive in public – i.e. 10th October 1987 – had still not resulted in the purchaser coming forward and there seemed little to be 'cautiously optimistic' about. There was not enough evidence against either of the Newall brothers, but no doubt the police were still hopeful that the strain would prove too great for Roderick – even if he was at the helm of the family yacht.

On Saturday, 8th October 1988, almost on the first anniversary of the Newalls' disappearance, David Ellam talked in considerable frustration to Philip Falle. The last year had been incredibly stressful for the Ellams as well as very frightening. Scarcely a day had gone by without the names of Nicholas and Elizabeth Newall being mentioned and both the Ellams, much to their annoyance, had become minor celebrities.

David Ellam said, 'I get angry when the police, the public and the press place such emphasis on finding the Newalls. Why don't people talk about finding the people who murdered them, that's what I want to know!'

The Ellams had always been convinced, like many others on the island, that Roderick and Mark had been involved in their parents' disappearance and Philip Falle hinted as much when he wrote in the *Jersey Evening Post*, 'David Ellam is convinced that the two strangers who became two friends have been murdered, just as he is convinced that more than one person was involved in the crime.'

Ellam continued, 'I have been questioned at length, had my fingerprints taken, had detectives in my home for days on end, so much so that I've sometimes wondered if the police think that Maureen and I killed them.

'I don't worry about that sort of thing, because if you have nothing to hide you have nothing to fear, but when I hear of people who might have either theories or information saying that they haven't told the police because they don't want to get involved, it makes my blood boil.

'It's not someone fiddling their tax that we're talking about, or getting something cheap that might possibly have been stolen.

'We are talking about people having been murdered and their killers are still walking around free. Not some petty little crime that will make you feel like a school sneak if you tell the police about it.'

David Ellam was possibly trying to bring matters to a head when the investigation was once again at an all-time low. His forthright attitude and rising impatience were all too understandable.

'For heaven's sake, whoever has information but doesn't want to get involved then I implore them to come forward, and either tell the police or tell me and I will tell the police.

'I know that there are occasions when it might well be embarrassing for a potential witness to come forward. None of us are perfect and perhaps there is someone out there who has information but was possibly somewhere where they should not have been, or with someone they should not have been.

'The police are both sensitive and discreet in these matters, but if you are that worried then ring me and talk about it.

'The people who have been killed are parents, they have mothers, sisters, brothers, nephews and nieces, as well as people like me, Maureen and their other friends, and to say that you don't want to get involved is a complete and utter abdication of your responsibility as a member of the human race, never mind your duty as a citizen.'

Ellam sounds almost apoplectic at this point, reflecting the frustration he must have felt at two new-found friends virtually disappearing off the face of the planet. Their 'non-existence' was a source of complete and continuous horror to the Ellams – a horror that didn't go away.

'I'm not one of these "I know what I'd do if I got my hands on 'em" brigade. If whoever did this needs to be punished, then that's a matter for the court, not for me, and if they need help, and anyone who does something like this does need help, then that's a matter for the court as well.

'What I want is to see them arrested, because I believe that once that happens then it's probable that two bodies will be found, and there will be an end to this suffering and uncertainty. We have given a lot of information to the police, but we don't know how much of it is useful and how much is useless, so being in that position does tend to make me worry, particularly about Maureen.'

But neither of the Ellams really went in fear of being murdered by Roderick Newall. In partnership with Philip Falle they were trying to voice their suspicions without making accusations they couldn't sustain. It was a delicate game.

David Ellam went on to imply that Kenneth Newall's coronary could well have been speeded up by the stress involved. 'These people are responsible for three deaths so far, and I say that quite deliberately, because I know how fond Nick's uncle in Sark, Kenneth Newall, was of them both, and his death just five weeks after they disappeared is as much attributable to their fate as if he, too, had been murdered.

'How many more people are going to suffer, and perhaps die before their time, before those who did this are brought before a court?

'There are times when I almost tear my hair out in frustration at the police, wondering why they have done this, or haven't done that, and then there are times when I have nothing but respect and admiration for what they have done, and some of the personal sacrifices I know from my own knowledge that many of them have made.

'There are times when I have the same sort of mixed feelings about Nick and Elizabeth's family. Should they perhaps have spent more time searching, digging holes, cajoling the police, making public appeals through the media?

'And then I think what they must be going through, and how they must feel with all this uncertainty, this not knowing, and then my heart goes out to them.'

Once again, David Ellam, in association with Philip Falle, was being careful. But Roderick Newall, if he had read the piece, would have been exceedingly concerned. Ellam continued, 'It just won't go away, no matter where I go, what I talk about, and who I meet. It is always there, either in the form of a tangible reminder – and there are plenty of those in our house – or as a topic of conversation once people know who I am and who used to live in our home.

'It seems a heartless, callous thing to think, never mind say; but I can't wait for the day when a policeman knocks at our door to tell us for certain that two friends are dead, because the bodies have been found.

'I only hope, for all our sakes, that the day is not too far away.'

94

On 9th September 1988, the sniffer dogs and their handlers from Lancashire Constabulary made a return to the island. In the previous March, they had found the items of clothing that almost certainly belonged to Nicholas and Elizabeth Newall, and now that the debris of the hurricane had largely been cleared it was felt that the dogs might make some more discoveries. The searches were being conducted on 'common land in the south', but the police did not want the exact locations revealed.

At the same time, Detective Chief Superintendent John Saunders returned to Jersey from Suffolk to examine the progress of the recommendations that he had made – and the intensifying of the search for the Newall bodies. The *Jersey Evening Post* reported on 9th September that 'the police are known to be keeping in touch with members of the Newall family including the couple's sons, Roderick and Mark, who were the last people to have seen their parents alive last October'. Was the net really closing in at last, or was this simply another false dawn?

Roderick, however, still sailing the *Chanson du Lecq* around the Mediterranean, whether a cold-blooded executioner or the hot-headed perpetrator of a *crime passionnel*, was not escaping from anything or anyone. He was taking the dreadful images of his parents' killings and the subsequent weeks of misery with him, whether he knew it or not. Perhaps he departed from Jersey more optimistically, convinced that the excitement of sailing would hold the grim memories at bay, even drown them, but soon the shadows of his slain parents returned to confront him. He must have imagined Nicholas or Elizabeth in their familiar positions at the helm as the *Chanson* cleaved her path through the waves – or seen them snug below decks. They were never to leave his conscience alone and his father's mental domination was to sap his spirit just as it always had. It would be difficult to banish his image completely, to be free from the suspicion that he was there beside him, furious that his erring son had not only murdered him but had taken his beloved sailing boat as well.

A highly competent sailor, however, Roderick, despite his terrible memories, would far rather face the high seas than the gathering suspicion in Jersey, and knowing the police couldn't contact him, he determined now he would sail for the Falkland Islands where he intended to start up his yacht-chartering business based on the expectancy of his parents' will. His experiences in the La Moye prison had made him acutely aware that eventually he might end up in there for life, and Roderick knew that was a fate that he couldn't bear and must avoid at all costs.

At twenty-three Roderick was a lone sailor with a difference. He had various plans to evade capture and was becoming both daring and resourceful. One plan he had in mind, once he had his hands on his share of Uncle Sark's money, was to do a 'Ronnie Biggs'. One of the 'Great Train Robbers', Biggs managed to get to Brazil where he fathered a child so that he could not be extradited. Roderick was determined, if necessary, to do the same, although he was now increasingly aware that wherever he went he was taking his dead parents with him.

7

On 19th December 1989, police investigations ceased at the Newalls' home in St Brelade; it was redecorated and some carpets replaced 'at public expense'. The head of the States police CID, Detective Chief Inspector Martyn Le Brocq, stated that the house was being handed back to the family. Advocate Le Quesne, however, had no idea when and neither would he say what would happen to the bungalow. His comment to the *Jersey Evening Post* was, 'I will probably be consulting Mr and Mrs Newall's sons to talk about that.'

For almost a year, despite rumours of a 'hired killer' emanating from speculation in the *Sunday Express* and the dragging of various ponds and waterways, the investigation lay fallow, and it was not until the death declaration was finally being prepared that the Newall murders surfaced again in the public consciousness.

Meanwhile, Mark was in New York and Roderick had arrived in the Falklands, working on the yacht, preparing it for charter. Soon he planned to sail for South America. It was three years since the Newalls had been murdered and any hope of a quick solution had now been ruled out. All the police could hope was that Roderick would either make a mistake or eventually be driven to confessing.

Advocate Le Quesne stated, 'I am in the process of drafting the necessary documents and my intention is to make application to the Royal Court for a declaration of death.' The documents were likely to have included a letter from Le Brocq to Le Quesne stating that, as a result of the detailed and prolonged enquiries made since the couple's disappearance in October 1987, the police were convinced they had met a violent death.

In the first week of November 1990, Advocate Le Quesne presented a representation on behalf of Roderick and Mark Newall stating that an application for a grant of probate on their parents' estate could not be pursued in the absence of death certificates because their bodies had not been found. Therefore in his opinion the court should make a declaration presuming death, providing it was satisfied with the evidence.

Mark Newall had agreed to be present when the Royal Court convened, but Roderick was still presumed to be in the Falklands. On 5th November 1990, when the court met for a brief preliminary hearing, it was agreed to substitute Roderick's name for that of a third executor to Nicholas Newall's will – barrister Peter Barnes, the son of Angela Barnes. Advocate Le Quesne told Sir Peter Crill, the Bailiff of Jersey, Chief Judge in the Royal Court, that Nicholas Newall had stipulated that his wife should be an executor of the will, but that in the event of her predeceasing him, Mr Barnes and Nicholas's two sons should be executors.

The court went on to order that Detective Chief Inspector Le Brocq should be called to attend the next hearing along with any police officers who had evidence to give and that the Attorney-General, Mr Philip Bailhache QC, should also be present.

On 13th November, the Royal Court heard that it might

be necessary for claims to be made against Nicholas Newall's estate because he was a member of a Lloyds underwriting syndicate, and the matter could not be properly handled until Nicholas was officially declared dead. The document went on to state that both Mark Newall and Peter Barnes believed the couple to be deceased, and since their disappearance Mark had been trying to look after the family business. The *Jersey Evening Post* reported that the document also stated that Roderick Newall was 'working on a vessel in or around the Falkland Islands and would be unlikely to be within easy reach of communication until early 1991'. Roderick had put up the walls of his island fortress and may well have decided at this time never to return home again.

On 3rd January 1991, the Royal Court officially presumed the Newalls dead and the bungalow was formally handed over to the estate.

According to the *Jersey Evening Post*, Mark 'sat pale-faced and with fists tightly clenched as forensic scientist David Northcott said he had concluded from his investigations that Nicholas Newall was probably killed in front of the fireplace of the lounge in his home. His wife had probably died in the master bedroom "just inside the door".' After the hearing, Mark Newall left without speaking to the ever-hopeful press, accompanied by the Newall family lawyer, Advocate David Le Quesne, and Detective Inspector Fitzgerald and Detective Inspector Adamson, two of the team of detectives who had been working for more than three years on the case which was now described in court as a murder enquiry. They went to Le Quesne's chambers where Mark was apparently 'briefed on what progress had been made in the investigation during the eighteen months or so since he last spoke to the police'.

Mark had told the court, 'I believe my parents are dead

primarily for three reasons. I have not seen or heard of them for three years; I have no evidence they have used any of their financial assets in those three years; and also largely because of evidence given to me by the police. They have indicated they are investigating murder.'

As a result of the court decision to hand over the bungalow, Mark Newall had the daunting task of walking into his parents' house for the first time since he had returned that evening to talk his brother out of suicide and to help him dispose of his parents' bodies.

Mark was joined by his dead mother's sister, Nan Clarke, and they both spent over an hour in the bungalow, accompanied by Detective Inspector Jim Adamson. When she left, Mrs Clarke was carrying a large black plastic sack, presumably containing some of the Newalls' belongings.

Later, Le Brocq confirmed that Mark had then spent some time with CID officers but he didn't want to comment on the conversation. He told the *Jersey Evening Post*, 'We wanted to talk to him because it has been about eighteen months since we last did so.'

On 4th May 1991, it was announced that Nicholas and Elizabeth Newall had left all their money and property on the island to their two sons. The will had been proved in the Probate Division of the Royal Court on Thursday, 18th April – six days before what would have been Nicholas's sixtieth birthday. However, there would be large claims from Lloyds on his particular estate.

Roderick's voyages in the *Chanson du Lecq* were enhanced, according to James Carr-Jones who sailed with him in 1989 off Panama, by marijuana and a double bed. Carr-Jones told the *Guardian*, 'He glassed in a kilo of marijuana in the boat and he'd had the whole of the front cabin converted into a double bed. Then he'd crossed the Atlantic with no wind. He had these photographs taken from the top of his mast. I suspect he spent a lot of time up the top of that mast, floating in the Atlantic, smoking the stuff.' According to Carr-Jones, Roderick had told him and another sailing companion, Madelon Treneman, that his parents had been murdered and he was unable to convince the police that he and his brother weren't involved. Carr-Jones continued, 'At the end of dinner one evening, I said to him "Did you do it?" He said, "Don't be silly." But he would bring up the subject of his parents' death as if he wanted to talk about it.' Treneman added, 'He didn't seem to care whether he was going to live or die. I always felt that his sailing trip was a way of challenging destiny. Either he was going to die or he would come back and start a new life. He was incredibly reckless, for example the marijuana in his boat, and then he had this plan to sail round Cape Horn in his small boat. The Cape is one of the most dangerous places in the world to sail, people told him he was mad. Once he'd got away with the murders, it was as if he'd decided to give life a try and if it didn't work and he died, that was fine.'

Falkland's Police Chief, Ken Greenland, said that his force had been aware of the investigations surrounding the disappearance of Roderick Newall's parents but he did not receive a special request from the Jersey police to keep an eye on him. Greenland remembered that Roderick had arrived in the Falklands around January 1990 and had worked as a deck hand on board the *Forrester* for some time.

'Although we did not keep a special eye on him, we knew of his general movements around the island, but as we only police Stanley it was difficult to keep track of him all the time and he was quite free to move around the islands.'

Sandy Enandas first met Roderick when she was a

passenger on the *Forrester* and was returning to the Falklands from South America. An attractive young woman in her early twenties, the two became close friends over Roderick's two-year period in the islands. She had been aware of the mystery surrounding his parents and he gave her some details. 'But I took this to mean that they had disappeared following an argument in a restaurant and had not been seen since.'

As a result of all these observations from those close to Roderick Newall at the time, it was becoming increasingly clear that he had a great longing to confess – but always stopped just short of the mark. At the same time he was still his attention-seeking, fun-loving self. During the Falkland Games held on Pebble Island in 1991 to celebrate the end of the lamb-shearing season, Roderick arrived unannounced in the *Chanson du Lecq*. He entered the two-mile cross-country run and won it – despite the fact that he had been smoking heavily. The manager of the Falklands Islands radio station, Patrick Watts, commented, 'After all, it's an achievement to sail to the Falklands but also it's still a place where you can easily get lost and disappear.'

En route to the Falklands from New Zealand he met Donna Westend, twenty-five and divorced, and she became his crew. She told the *Telegraph* that their relationship was tempestuous. 'He is quick tempered and I can be quite fiery too. I possibly suspected something. You cannot be a normal person carrying a secret like that. He had reasons for doing what he did and it is not for me to judge him. We were from worlds apart, but I will never forget him.' Neither will yachtsman Gerome Poncet, whom Roderick stayed with for some months on Beaver Island. Poncet told the London *Evening Standard*, 'Roderick was wonderful with my children and was always saying how he was never loved as a child. It was obvious he wanted children of his own to bring them up the right way and right what he saw as a wrong done to him. I had a lot of sympathy for him, but to be honest you don't kill your parents because they sent you to boarding school.'

But Roderick didn't do that. Rejection was only a foundation for murder. Uncle Sark's money must have provided an additional motive.

Mark had phoned Roderick and told him that their parents had been declared dead and that they had both inherited the fortune shortly before he arrived at the Beleiros Sol Yacht Club at Poro Alegre in Brazil. There he met Elena Pedo, separated and with two young children, who invited him to the thirtieth birthday party of a friend, Eloise Endres. Roderick took both women out for a dinner with champagne and told them, 'I have become a millionaire today.' But even as he was uttering these words, Roderick must have cast his mind back to the dinner at the Sea Crest Hotel restaurant in Jersey and its traumatic aftermath.

Roderick told Elena he was on his way back to the Falklands and that he had wanted to go round the world in his yacht. Roderick also told her that he was heir to a fortune (Lloyds' claims on Nicholas had ceased with his death as he had taken out an insurance to this effect) but on closer acquaintance she found him to be frightened and uneasy.

A month later, *en route* back to the Falklands, he sold the *Chanson du Lecq*. This must have been done either to try to absolve its memories or to get a larger vessel that would be better suited to the charter operation he envisaged. In the interim he and Elena flew to Buenos Aires and in January 1992 they flew on to Miami where Roderick hoped to buy the replacement yacht; apparently his search was unsuccessful.

Although his friendship with Elena brought him considerable comfort, he was now so obsessed with guilt that he was finding day-to-day life increasingly difficult to maintain. He was probably ready to confess now; whatever the consequences, Roderick knew he had to be free of his appalling burden, the albatross that had pursued him from Jersey.

The moment came when he and Elena went to see *Cape Fear* starring Robert de Niro in Miami. The film concluded with the words, 'If you hang on to the past, you'll die a little every day.' That's exactly what Roderick must have felt.

Elena Pedo claimed that she hated the violence in the film but Roderick loved it. 'I love living with fear,' he had apparently told her. After the cinema she alleged he broke down and confessed, telling her the police knew he had killed his parents. Later, she alleged, Roderick had asked her to read from *Magister Ludi* by Hermann Hesse, which read, 'Oh! he thought in grief and horror, now I am guilty of his death. And only now, when there was no longer need to save his pride or offer resistance, he felt, in shock and sorrow, how dear this man had already become to him.' When she had finished reading, Roderick, she claimed, broke down in tears and then grabbed her by the shoulders, shaking her, shouting hysterically, 'I'm a murderer.' But Elena said she didn't accept what she had heard and, as time went by, she believed in the confession less and less.

It was only much later, when Elena's name and telephone number were discovered in Roderick's address book after his arrest at sea, that she was contacted by the police and eventually two plain-clothes officers from Jersey flew out to interview her.

After his confession to Elena, Roderick must have felt a sense of relief, but it was not to last long for nothing could alleviate the continuous replay of how he had murdered his parents. He must also have kept rerunning Mark's arrival at the bungalow, his slow talking down and then the frantic dumping of the bodies, their subsequent burial and the botched attempt to clean up the rooms.

The continuous trauma mounted in his mind, besieging both sleeping and waking moments. The rice flail making contact with his father's – and then his mother's – head, the spiralling and swamping blood, and the stillness of the corpses. However much they had obsessed him with their mutual absorption, however much he had suffered when Nicholas and Elizabeth had sent him away, they were still his all-too-familiar parents. And he had killed them. Like the characters in Jean-Paul Sartre's *Huis Clos*, who repeated and repeated a part of their lives in hell, Roderick was doing the same with the events of the night of 10th October. He had murdered his parents, and whether he was at sea or on land, despite his confession to Elena, the memories haunted him until he could think of nothing else. La Moye prison and its confines had now become a dim memory and Roderick decided to return to England.

His motives will probably never be known but it is possible that he had a longing to see his Uncle Stephen – his father's twin brother. Perhaps he thought that by talking to him – even confessing – he might in some mysterious way persuade him to intervene on his behalf. The nightmare memories in the wilderness had clearly become intolerable and even if he didn't want to confess to Stephen Newall, maybe he wanted to return to those familiar shores and try to test himself out against the ghosts of his parents. Either way, Roderick Newall arrived in June 1992, ostensibly to complete the purchase and take delivery of his much sought new yacht, the *Austral Soma*. He had always kept in touch with his grandmother [Elizabeth's mother, Mrs Nelson], and usually he and Mark maintained contact through her with the rest of the family and even between themselves. In fact, the Jersey police had been able to keep a check on his movements in the South Atlantic as he often sent Mrs Nelson flowers on his MasterCard.

The next move was when Nancy Clarke, Elizabeth's sister, phoned Angela Barnes in Jersey to say that Roderick had visited her at her Fulham house, stating that he was going up to Scotland to see Stephen and Gaye Newall and that, at one point, they spoke about mediums. Nancy told him that she 'had been sent a message through a friend of Elizabeth's'. Roderick asked Nancy if his mother had ever appeared to her and she said, 'Yes, the night she died.' He then asked Nancy what Elizabeth had said and she replied that she had had a bizarre nightmare on the night his parents had died. She dreamt she had seen her sister's funeral and told the *Telegraph*, 'I heard the sound of horses' hooves. We were in the car and ahead of us was a black, horse-drawn carriage. I saw Nicholas sitting smiling on the seat at the back, and there were two postilions with wizened faces. I said: "Where's Elizabeth?" The carriage stopped and Elizabeth got out. I can see her face now. She was resigned, not bitter or mad. She shrugged and said, "I told you what was going to happen. Just let it be." I shouted to her to wait but I never finished the dream. My husband, Alister, woke me because I was shouting.'

Nancy told Roderick that despite this she still wanted to know what had happened. Her nephew then said to her, 'Even if you knew exactly what happened, you would still not understand.' Nancy urged, 'Why would I not understand?' and Roderick replied, 'I don't understand why myself.' Nancy explained to Angela how she had told Roderick over dinner that she had had the visitation from Elizabeth on the night she had died and had become suspicious when Roderick did not question which night that was. As a result, Nancy believed that he was on the point of confessing something.

It seemed strange that she did not immediately confide in the police, but perhaps she still did not want to admit, even to herself, that Roderick could have been implicated in the murder of her sister and brother-in-law. Instead, she made the call to Angela Barnes, who was also doubtful about what course of action should be taken. In turn, she rang Maureen Ellam, and as a result of this conversation Angela was left in no doubt as to what she had to do. She called the police.

When Roderick arrived in London and made contact with Nancy Clarke, he also saw a friend, Emma Jane Lonsdale, who let him stay at her London flat and borrow her blue Golf GTI in which he drove to Scotland where he stayed at his grandmother's house.

Meanwhile, the Jersey States police, having been tipped off by Angela Barnes, asked their colleagues in the Scottish Crime Squad to check the Golf was outside Mrs Nelson's house. They were able to identify the number plate which had been noted by the resourceful Nancy Clarke. When the Jersey States police rang Mrs Clarke it became clear how suspicious she had become. Not only did she indicate that Roderick might be on the point of confession but she admitted that she had been so concerned by his behaviour that she had taken the number of the GTI. As a result the Scottish police made a correct identification and were able to put Roderick under surveillance.

Stephen Newall then rang Mrs Nelson's home. He had been contacted by the Jersey police and also by Nancy Clarke who told him Roderick wanted to see him. Stephen invited him for tea at the Dunkeld House Hotel the following day, 14th July 1992, at 3 p.m.

Tape-recorded evidence can be a legal minefield but Superintendent Paul Marks secured Stephen Newall's permission to bug the conversation between him, his wife and his nephew in room number 138, making clear to Stephen the necessity of not personally encouraging any statement from Roderick. Whatever his nephew said had to be both spontaneous and of his own volition; there were to be no leading questions.

These ominous instructions put both Stephen and Gaye under considerable strain. For the first hour after Roderick had arrived, with the detectives positioned a few rooms away, listening and recording, no mention was made of the disappearance of Nicholas and Elizabeth Newall. Stephen then referred to the conversation Roderick had had three days earlier with Nancy and what he had said to her. The conversation then became very emotional with Roderick saying a number of things to his uncle and aunt that amounted to a confession to being involved in the murder of his parents in October 1987. Superintendent Paul Marks takes up the story in his own words, as told to Philip Falle.

'The technical people put a tape recorder with a three-hour tape under one of the chairs and just before Roderick was due to arrive that was to be switched on. There was no control over the tape and when it had to be replaced something had to divert him.'

As Marks and Adamson approached the hotel they were warned on the radio of their unmarked car that Roderick Newall was behind them, heading for the same destination. His VW Golf was heading fast for the same roundabout and the police officers were told to pull in at the gates of a big brewery down the road where the Crime Squad would join them. There they were challenged by the gatekeeper who didn't believe they were police officers and called out the local police.

'By the time they arrived the Crime Squad came screaming in to the gate area and picked us up, transferred cars, and we joined their part of the operation. We were able to listen over the radio, literally following him (Roderick) into the hotel area.

'As he was turning in to the gate someone said "He's stopped, hold back" and we thought, that's it, it's blown out, he's not going to go in. He got out, changed his shirt, got back in and drove up the drive to the hotel front door and went in.

'We had to go in through the back of the hotel. We were listening to the commentary. We heard commentary which included what was going on in the room, so we knew that he'd arrived, that Stephen had gone downstairs to pick him up, that he'd come back and was in the room. The commentary said "go back, he's leaving the room". He came out of the room, went down to the car, picked up something from the car and returned. What that was was the brochure for the yacht.

'Once they were settled back in the room and we were confident that he wasn't going to leave again, because the conversation was going well between the uncle and aunt and Roderick, we crept up to where the surveillance was being monitored. To get to it we actually passed the door of the suite, very much on tiptoe. There were four of us, and we went into the room from where the operation was going to be commanded . . .

'We settled in and started listening to the conversation. It went on for about 50-odd minutes with innocent chatter about where he'd been, what he'd done, how many miles he'd sailed his boat round the world, to the Antipodes, South America, the Falklands, what his business plans were for the coming summer, the purchase of the *Austral Soma*, which was an expensive piece of kit, from the proceeds of the estate. Jimmy was sitting down listening to it all and making notes.

'I must admit that at that stage I was beginning to get some funny looks from these people [the Scottish Crime Squad officers]. They'd cancelled what was quite an important operation for them and supplied us with all this kit and they were beginning to wonder whether it was actually going to come to anything.'

Marks and Adamson had arranged with Gaye and Stephen Newall that although on no account must they ask leading questions when 'tea was ordered and brought would be an ideal time to say that Nan had rung and said something rather strange about "you wouldn't understand, even if you knew". That was an agreed trigger to try and get the subject round . . .

'He [Roderick] broke down as soon as he [Stephen] asked him what he meant and I know now why he did it because when you look at the evidence of Miss [Elena] Pedo because she said his one fear, after the confession to her, months before, was of going home and looking into the eyes of his uncle and being unable to hold back the tears. He told her that in Brazil, when he was down there the previous summer. So he wanted to unburden himself, and maybe reconcile himself with his uncle, who he greatly admired . . .

'I think his mission was to come to terms with it by talking to him. I think that's why he went there. In that sense it was completely voluntary. It was not dragged out of him, he wanted to do it and he did it. He was pretty clever in the way he did it though, because he was very cryptic by using words which even witnesses if they turned against him to do their duty . . . if they were going to repeat what he was saying it would have been extremely difficult, given the way he failed to complete sentences, or invariably half said things which left understandings but not the words which were used. But as the conversation went on it was pretty clear that first of all a lot had happened, secondly that he was feeling remorse, and he did feel a burden of responsibility to them. He spoke around it for some considerable time.

'But it was a confession, there was no doubt about it. At the end of the day it was a confession that didn't use the traditional words of a confession. It wasn't a confession that a policeman would have helped somebody to put on paper. It was a completely natural, for him, way of trying to communicate to his uncle that he had done it and that he had suffered as a result, that it was very, very difficult to live with.

'I believe that it was such compelling stuff that they [Stephen and Gaye] forgot we were there. At one stage he really was talking so naturally. It was an uncle/nephew relationship and I felt I was listening to a private conversation.

'Stephen actually took a grip of himself in a way. The other thing I had told him was that if it progressed to a point where the bodies could be recovered, it would be quite reasonable for him to try to find out where they were . . .

'We then had a wicked sort of situation in terms of admissibility because he started to describe the graves and while that was very interesting I didn't want them described, I wanted to know where they were, but I was very relieved in a way to know that there was a grave there. That there was a grave. Because he described the problems associated with getting the bodies back, because of plastic. Bells were beginning to ring in terms of knowledge of the case because I knew that press releases about the plastic had come out. Relatively well camouflaged, could be found, the use of modern technology, but he did not say where they were.'

At that point the tape needed changing, so Stephen had the presence of mind to take Gaye and Roderick for a walk in the hotel grounds. When they returned, 'the conversation resumed, and it suddenly ended, quite quickly. Roderick had been through this experience, job done, I'm on my way. It was just like that, and we were back to nephew and uncle, and the parting shot was I've brought you a little present for your birthday, and it was little, just like he gave his mother a present, on the night of the murder, and he was off. He walked out and back to his car.'

Elements of the confession were fully reported later in Gibraltar when Desmond de Silva QC outlined the case during Roderick Newall's extradition proceedings. The salient points, however, were as follows:

(1) His parents' bodies were in plastic and were camouflaged.
(2) That he carried the blame for this equally with another.
(3) That there were no mitigating circumstances for what he had done.
(4) That if the police moved in on him there existed a suicide pact with his accomplice.
(5) That it was not going to help by him sitting in prison for 25 years for the stigma was likely to finish off his grandmother.
(6) That if he was a Catholic he would seek absolution.
(7) That he was quite looking forward to seeing his parents 'on the far side'.
 Uncle: 'to say you are sorry'
 Roderick: 'No'

(8) When his uncle suggested to Roderick that there would not be much evidence on the bodies now Roderick replied that they would have definite clothes on which would, to use his words, 'pin it down to a night'. We say "it" refers to the killing.

(9) Then having told his uncle that he needed to get legal advice Roderick said to his uncle 'I don't think I'd mind too much paying the price' and that for the sake of the family he wanted the matter cleared up.

When Stephen eventually brought up the most obvious question of all, 'Why?', Roderick's enigmatic reply had been, 'You wouldn't understand because I don't understand.'

The police would no doubt have wanted to arrest Roderick Newall immediately after the interview with his aunt and uncle, and the hotel was already swarming with officers of the Scottish Crime Squad, but the police in Scotland told their Jersey counterparts that, without a warrant, they could only hold Roderick for a matter of hours.

As soon as the three-hour conversation between Roderick, Stephen and Gaye was over, Marks rang Jersey's Attorney-General and Director of Public Prosecutions, Philip Bailhache, for further instructions. Over the last five years, Bailhache had continuously dampened the spirits of many enthusiastic policemen in Jersey for he had never been convinced that there was enough evidence to put before a jury – and even now, despite Marks' detailed resumé of the conversation between Roderick and his uncle and aunt, Bailhache remained cautious, certain that he still could not sanction a warrant from Jersey's Bailiff, Sir Peter Crill, until he had heard the contents of the tape himself.

The delay was to give Roderick a considerable head-start

for he was now heading south in Emma Jane Lonsdale's Golf GTI, followed by the police. It was probably while he was on the M6 that Roderick Newall realised he was being tailed, and for the first time since he had disposed of his parents' bodies his army experience came in useful. As he came off the M6 where it joins the M62 at Warrington, he was able to confirm that he was being tailed. Experienced policemen know that it is comparatively easy to follow a suspect on a motorway, hiding in lanes of fast moving traffic, overtaking and being overtaken, but they dread roundabouts. Roderick must have known this from his anti-surveillance training in the Royal Green Jackets. He drove round twice, made sure his tail was in the wrong position and then streaked off, losing them completely.

Eventually, Roderick drove the Golf back to Emma Jane Lonsdale's flat, left a gift for her and telephoned his aunt in Fulham at 2.30 p.m. on Wednesday, 15th July. He told her that he would not be able to visit her and explained he had been 'followed' on the way back from Scotland. He then told her he was going to France to meet his boat. At the same time as this call, Jersey police officers were meeting the Attorney-General at a Special Branch office at Heathrow Airport where the Attorney-General listened to parts of the 'confession' recordings. Two days later, on 17th July, a warrant was issued for Roderick Newall's arrest. Meanwhile, Roderick had driven his own car back to Dover, crossing to Boulogne in whose harbour the *Austral Soma* was moored. Later, Emma Jane received a note from Roderick sent privately from Paris and then posted in London franked 6th August. It read: 'See you in Brazil, but only time will tell.' Possibly Mark had met his brother in Boulogne and been given the letter to send off from Paris. The wording must refer to the idea that Roderick had previously had: if, like Ronnie Biggs the train robber, he fathered a child in Brazil then the Jersey authorities would probably find the task of extraditing him very difficult indeed.

Once more on the high seas Roderick must have experienced a lessening of tension. The recollections of La Moye prison were behind him and now that he had told his father's twin brother at least some of the truth, he could well have felt tremendous relief. But his catharsis was not to last long for the police now had what they needed – the warrant for Roderick's arrest.

8

As the *Austral Soma* left Boulogne, rounded the Cherbourg peninsula and continued on between the French coast and the Channel Islands, a press black-out was instituted. Mark, meanwhile, had been making plans of his own. His career, despite the pressures of the last few years, had taken off to a very high degree.

Now based in Paris, he commuted between there and New York. In Paris he had a chaffeur-driven white BMW and a two-storey, two-bedroomed apartment with a roof garden. In New York he had an apartment overlooking Central Park. When he was eventually arrested in 1993 he had a six-figure salary as well as a fund that gave him an additional income of £150,000 a year. He is believed to have received a £200,000 pay-off from his employers after his arrest, with an option of a £100,000-a-year job on his release. To say the least, Mark had fallen on his feet, but there could be no doubt that the strain he was under was every bit as arduous as Roderick's.

At the end of July he had discussed with Roderick how long it would take him to sail to North Africa. Now, he flew to London from Paris and checked in at his favourite hotel, Blakes. In the early hours of 30th July, Mark dialled a number which was immediately passed on to the Jersey police, as by this time he was under surveillance by officers from Scotland Yard and arrangements had been made to have his calls from the hotel monitored. DS Charlie Mac-Dowall later called the number which turned out to be the offices of Air France in Los Angeles. After identifying himself, MacDowall established that Mark had booked a flight from Heathrow to Tangier; he was assumed to be meeting his brother. Investigating officers suspected that Mark had been in the UK to collect the *Austral Soma*'s registration papers that Roderick needed before he could start his business in the South Atlantic.

Although it has its own parliament, the States, and is responsible for its own internal affairs, responsibility for Jersey's defence and overseas representation is vested in HM Government in the UK, and it was for this reason that the request for the arrest of Roderick Newall had to be made through official diplomatic channels. As a result the Home Office asked a Royal Navy ship in the region of Gibraltar to help in the search for the *Austral Soma*.

Mark, meanwhile, was on his way to Tangier in what was to be his last face-to-face meeting with Roderick until they met in La Moye prison fifteen months later. Mark only stayed a few hours there and was soon on his way back to Paris, but in all probability he gave his brother sufficient funds for the provisioning of the *Austral Soma* for the long voyage to the Falklands. The two brothers must also have taken a very emotive farewell from each other. Roderick must have known by now that he was on the run and Mark must have been terrified at the prospect of the police being apparently so near but, they both imagined, still so far. The Newall brothers were wrong, however, for once Roderick left Tangier he was a marked man.

The press black-out – designed to ensure Roderick had no idea he was still being pursued – ran from the time when he went to Scotland to see his uncle until Friday, 7th August 1992, when the Royal Navy frigate HMS *Argonaut* intercepted the *Austral Soma* and Roderick was arrested 150 miles south-west of Gibraltar as he sailed towards the Canary Islands on his way to the Falklands.

HMS *Argonaut*, which was not part of the regular Mediterranean fleet but had been visiting Gibraltar, picked up the *Austral Soma* on its radar on Monday, 3rd August as the yacht left Tangier. Supported by patrol craft HMS *Ranger*, the *Argonaut* made a positive identification before retreating over the horizon to make sure she was unseen. At first the frigate tailed the *Austral Soma* to ensure she was going to remain in international waters and then, still using radar as well as her two Sea Lynx helicopters, continued to follow the yacht for another forty-eight hours. On board the frigate were police from both Jersey and Gibraltar.

Unfortunately for Roderick, the *Austral Soma* was flying the Red Ensign, which meant that she was British-registered and the *Argonaut* had a right to arrest her. Had she been flying a French or Spanish flag she would have been allowed to continue on to the Canaries. Once again, as in the too hurried cleaning up of the bungalow, Roderick Newall's planning had been faulty.

To his surprise he was then contacted on the *Argonaut*'s radio and asked to come aboard her and present his papers. Initially he was unwilling to co-operate, but after further communication Roderick was convinced that HMS *Argonaut* was only conducting stop-and-search operations. Little realising what was awaiting him on board, he rowed over in a small dinghy to be greeted by Detective Sergeant Charles MacDowall of the States of Jersey police. Also on board were Inspector Louis Wink and a number of other officers of the Royal Gibraltar Police who were armed with service revolvers and automatic weapons.

On boarding, Roderick Newall was met by Lieutenant J. Wardle and led to the centre of the flight deck where he was confronted by the Gibraltar Police Special Weapons team and DS MacDowall. Roderick was told to raise his hands but he refused to obey the officer's instructions. He was then told to lie on the deck but he also refused to comply with this. It was found necessary for him to be 'placed' on the deck where DS MacDowall showed him the Jersey warrant. Roderick Newall was then formally arrested for the murder of his parents in 1987.

Captain Robert Stevens, the frigate's commanding officer, told the *Jersey Evening Post* on the same day, 'He [Roderick] was amazed. He was taken totally by surprise to see a Jersey police officer aboard any vessel. To be quite frank, he was speechless.'

Roderick was horrified. Because of the successful press black-out, he had had no idea that a warrant had been taken out and to be stopped at sea rather than on the M62 in the UK was not something he had reckoned with.

Advocate David Le Quesne gave Mark's reaction from his office at the Banque Arabe et Internationale d'Investisse-ment in Paris, stating that he 'is surprised by his brother's arrest – as we all are.' Le Quesne added, 'If the police want to talk to Mark, all they have to do is to pick up the phone and call me.'

One of Roderick's closest friends, Emma Hadfield from Cambridge, was reported by the *Daily Express* on 7th August as saying, 'I'm totally shocked by this. Rod is a fantastic guy.' The *Express* went on to report that Emma Hadfield was 'a scientist with the British Antarctic Survey. She met Newall three years ago in the Falklands, where she was doing field work and he interrupted a round-the-world voyage. They often sailed together. She said she had not seen Newall for a couple of months but was determined to contact him in Gibraltar to lend her support.'

A handling crew from the *Argonaut* was then put on board the *Austral Soma* and all three vessels returned to Gibraltar with their prisoner apparently held at gunpoint. Roderick's reputation had clearly gone before him. On the voyage back he told MacDowall that when he had first seen the police firearms officers on the flight deck he had considered making a grab for one of the weapons which he identified as being an MP5. He added that he had assessed he could take four rounds before it stopped him. He also said that if he had realised what was about to happen on boarding the Naval boat he would probably have rammed the frigate.

Once in Gibraltar, Roderick indicated to police officers that he would take the quick option to return to Jersey and would not oppose extradition as he did not want to cause further distress to his family. But he changed his mind.

Roderick Newall was remanded in the custody of the Gibraltar police. As a result the Jersey authorities had only a week to present the case for him to be extradited to the Jersey courts. If this was granted, he would then have fifteen days in which to appeal.

It is not absolutely clear why HMS *Argonaut* did not return Roderick Newall direct to the island, but it is likely that the warship could not be permitted to leave her current operational area. Clearly the Jersey officials were disappointed and Chief Inspector Bill Danino of the Gibraltar police commented that Roderick, now twenty-seven, would only be quickly returned to Jersey if the evidence against him was not challenged. Danino added, 'If it is not, it could take just two or three weeks, but if he does contest it, it could take up to a year. The last one took eleven months and that was for a less serious charge.'

Once again, it looked as if Roderick was going to get some breathing space and his cat-and-mouse game with the authorities in Jersey would continue.

During his brief appearance in the Gibraltar court, he made only one statement: 'I was arrested by Jersey officers on the high seas and brought to Gibraltar at gunpoint.' A spokesman for Newall added that the manner of his arrest had been 'outrageous at bringing him back at gunpoint' and that there had been many opportunities to interview him over the past five years.

Roderick then hired a top Gibraltar lawyer named Chris Finch who had acted for the families of the three IRA members shot dead in the colony by British security forces and who was also an ex-policeman. Finch was highly experienced and through him Roderick planned to appeal for bail. For the moment however he was confined to the cells of the Moorish Castle prison which must have brought back painful memories of his incarceration at La Moye – a stark and claustrophobic contrast to his life at sea.

The Jersey police chief, David Parkinson, issued this statement:

In mid-October 1987, Nicholas Newall and his wife, Elizabeth, disappeared from their home in St Brelade, Jersey, and on 18 October 1987, they were formally reported to police in Jersey as missing persons.

There followed a protracted and intense police enquiry, during which the States of Jersey police came to the conclusion that the couple had been murdered in their home, and despite the fact that they or their bodies have never been traced, on the third day of January

1991, in the Royal Court of Jersey, the court declared that the deaths of Nicholas Newall and Elizabeth, his wife, were presumed beyond all reasonable doubt to have occurred between 11 and 18 October 1987.

The police enquiry has never been closed, but following the initial investigations the evidence obtained has been reviewed and, with the assistance of the Devon and Cornwall Constabulary, has been transferred on to the HOLMES computer.

As a result of new developments, a further review of that evidence has been undertaken in more recent times, led by the head of the CID, Detective Superintendent Marks. This review involved two senior officers, Inspector Martin Fitzgerald and Inspector James Adamson, who had taken part in the original police investigation.

Following the issue of the warrant, assistance was sought from Interpol, the Metropolitan Police and provincial police forces in England and a number of other police forces and agencies throughout the world to trace Roderick Newall, whose whereabouts were unknown, in order to effect his arrest.

During the weekend of 1 and 2 August 1992, and as a result of these enquiries, Detective Inspector James Adamson and Detective Sergeant Charles MacDowall travelled to Gibraltar, where the assistance of the Gibraltar police was obtained and, at the same time, a request was made through HM Lieut. Governor in Jersey to the Home Office and Ministry of Defence in London, to enable the assistance of HM Navy based in Gibraltar to be granted to the Jersey officers.

During the early morning of Wednesday, 5 August, ships of HM Royal Navy, namely HMS *Argonaut*, a frigate, and HMS *Ranger*, a patrol craft, with Detective Sergeant Charles MacDowall of the Jersey police aboard, located the British-registered yacht *Austral Soma*, owned by Roderick Newall, in international waters *en route* for the Canary Islands. The yacht was stopped late yesterday afternoon and officers of the Gibraltar police in the company of Detective Sergeant Mac-Dowall, armed with the warrant of arrest, effected the arrest of Roderick Newall.

Roderick Newall, together with the yacht *Austral Soma* and other unidentified crew members, were then escorted back to Gibraltar, where an application for the extradition of Roderick Newall to Jersey will be carried out. It is believed that Roderick will be appearing before the Gibraltar court today.

The investigation which is continuing is now being led by Assistant Chief Officer Simpson, and a further statement will be issued in due course.

I wish to place on record my deep appreciation and thanks to the local media, who, although aware of recent increased police activity, agreed that no details would be published, as any publicity would have jeopardised what has been an extremely delicate operation. The media acknowledged the sensitivity of the operation and displayed their highest professional standards throughout with their responsible attitude.

I also wish to extend my grateful thanks to the Commissioner and members of the Gibraltar police, the Ministry of Defence in general and Her Majesty's Royal Navy in particular, and other agencies, too numerous to mention, for their full co-operation and unstinting support in bringing this phase of the investigation to a successful conclusion.

Although it sounded as if Parkinson was thanking the hard-working stall-holders of a small church fête, the summing-up came as a tremendous relief to a large number of frustrated police officers in Jersey – as well as to Nicholas and Elizabeth's friends and relations. It was, however, premature, for Roderick Newall was currently marshalling all his considerable resources to challenge the evidence being prepared against him.

Meanwhile, the press flocked to Gibraltar, anxious to interview the captain and ship's company of HMS *Argonaut*. NICKED BY THE NAVY, said the *Daily Star*, and the *Mirror* screamed BERGERAC MURDER: SON SEIZED BY THE NAVY. SURRENDER ON THE HIGH SEAS said *Today*, while sub-headlines raved NAVY FRIGATE STALKS MURDER PROBE SON and MURDER MYSTERY ON TAX EXILE ISLAND THAT IS LIKE A PLOT FROM TV BERGERAC.

Most of the hacks found Gibraltarians singularly unmoved. There were, in effect, two communities in Gibraltar, the military and the civilian. The military, in the shape of the Royal Navy, were delighted that the operation to locate and stop the *Austral Soma* was successful, but the media attention that centred on the arrest of Roderick Newall went largely unnoticed by the people of Gibraltar itself – despite the fact that the following day Roderick Newall's arrest on suspicion of the murder of his parents in Jersey made headline news in the colony's only newspaper, the *Gibraltar Chronicle*. Nevertheless, the topics of conversation among those who gathered in the many bars and cafés were more concerned with the death of the Rock's only cow and the forthcoming social event of the year, Miss Gibraltar 1992.

The attitude of the civilian community can best be summed up by the stance taken by the *Chronicle*, which carried no pictures of Newall arriving at the Gibraltar magistrates' court – despite the fact that the prison van had to stop in the narrow main street outside the court and the prisoners were walked through a small forest of palm trees and tropical plants.

Most of the reporters sent to Gibraltar by their editors were, in fact, show business writers dragged away from neighbouring Spain, where they had been following the doubtful fortunes of the BBC's doomed soap opera *Eldorado*. When they arrived, seeking to purchase photographs of Roderick Newall for their papers, they were told that the *Chronicle*'s only photographer was covering a flower show at the time of the court case. Pictures of that meant far more to their readership than the arrest of a yachtsman by a Royal Navy frigate more than a hundred miles away.

Meanwhile, down at the docks, the Navy had laid on coffee and biscuits for the press, and the skippers of HMS *Argonaut* and HMS *Ranger* gave a conducted tour of the pier at which those vessels and the *Austral Soma* were berthed. Previously, there had been dire warnings from the Ministry of Defence press liaison officer, Captain Leo Callow of the Royal Irish Rangers, not to ask any questions concerning the tracking and eventual boarding of the yacht and which forms of surveillance were used.

Captain Rob Stevens spoke to the press in the wardroom of the *Argonaut*, and describing the operation in as much detail as he was allowed he went on to mention his own ship's company.

'The crew were superb. We had given most of them shore leave, and only a few remained on board. Yet we were able to sail with almost a full complement less than four hours after the request for assistance came through. They did the job to perfection, which did not surprise me at all, for if you give people a real job to do, as opposed to training and exercises, they will do it and enjoy it.' Royal Navy propaganda apart, however, the *Argonaut* had done singularly well to find and then follow the *Austral Soma* amongst so many other yachts in the area.

Nan Clarke flew out to Gibraltar and Steve Beldham, now discovered to be the only member of crew on board the *Austral Soma*, was released and arrived at Gibraltar airport to take a flight to London. He refused to comment on either Roderick Newall or his arrest.

Until evidence and response could be collected together, not even the police could see Roderick, which was particularly frustrating in view of the dramatic arrest at sea.

In the week of 10th August, Jersey's Attorney-General, Mr Philip Bailhache, travelled to Gibraltar along with Detective Inspector Jim Adamson and Detective Sergeant Charles MacDowall, who had been on HMS *Argonaut* with Detective Inspector Louis Wink of the Gibraltar police, to attend the second appearance of Roderick Newall in the magistrates' court. They were needed by the magistrate, Felix Pizzarello, who was certain he was going to receive a draft application from Roderick's lawyer, Chris Finch, for bail – which the Jersey team intended to oppose vigorously. The formal extradition proceedings were expected to start in September and the application was to be presented by Gibraltar's new Attorney-General, John Blackburn-Gittings. If Roderick and his legal advisers were to fight this then the magistrate had to find that there was a prima facie case for Roderick Newall to answer before he could order his extradition to Jersey.

Bailhache told the *Jersey Evening Post* on 18th August that even if the hearings were protracted he was determined that Newall, who was arrested on a warrant alleging that he murdered his parents in October 1987, would stand trial. 'I am confident that Roderick Newall will be returned to Jersey,' he said. Nevertheless, Bailhache must have wondered if he had been too cautious about wanting to hear the vital tape himself. If he had been able to issue the warrant earlier, Roderick would not have been able to put to sea.

9

Ably supported by his lawyer, Roderick Newall then proceeded to exert every effort to fight the extradition order. He began by asserting that the arrest by HMS *Argonaut* was not tenable, but Gittings responded by stating, 'The High Court in England has held that it does not matter in what circumstances a wanted person is returned to the jurisdiction, and there are a number of cases to support this view.' He added that in his experience the Newall case was in many respects unique and was likely to be the most publicised hearing in Gibraltar since the inquest four years ago into the deaths of the IRA members shot by the SAS.

Roderick Newall was then remanded in custody for a week by Pizzarello. He made no bail application and was silent in the dock for the whole of the nine-minute hearing.

Chris Finch thought there should be reporting restrictions but Gittings argued that he had a duty to tell the court why the defendant was there. After pointing out that Newall was 'wanted for two murders', Gittings said, 'No one knows at this stage that there is any evidence against him. He could be as innocent as the driven snow. It looks like justice behind closed doors. We do not know what happened on 10th October 1987, and we do not know what happened on 14th July 1992.'

Chris Finch, who was now accompanied by the Newall family's Jersey lawyer, Advocate David Le Quesne, repeated again that anything said in court could be prejudicial to a fair trial, but Gittings continued to contend that 'everyone has a right to know'.

After the hearing, both Gittings and Bailhache expressed delight. 'As far as we were concerned it went perfectly,' said Gittings. They had achieved what they wanted – a custodial remand – and Roderick and Chris Finch had lost the first round. Bailhache then returned to Jersey to prepare the case for extradition.

By 20th August, with Roderick continually remanded in custody, he heard Magistrate Pizzarello set 17th September 1992 as the date for the formal hearing and, once again, there was no application for bail. Philip Falle wrote in the *Jersey Evening Post* on 20th August, 'Newall sat on the court bench just a few inches from the front row of the public gallery, his eyes fixed rigidly on the empty witness stand as Mr Gittings applied for a remand in custody for a further week and for a date to be set for the formal extradition hearing.' Meanwhile, Chris Finch continued to find as many technical obstacles as he could, including once again challenging the validity of the arrest on board HMS *Argonaut*.

Pizzarello reserved his judgment for a week on the counsel's submission that the arrest was unlawful and the warrant should be revoked to allow Roderick his freedom. Finch declared that the document referred to the defendant having 'absconded' which was quite untrue, as after the enquiry into his parents' death some years had passed and Newall 'did not go back, nor was he asked to go back'.

Using Gibraltar's Fugitive Offenders Act, Finch stated

that a warrant should only be issued in the colony when a person was either in jurisdiction or deemed to be on his way there. He went on to say that Newall was *en route* to the Canary Islands and not Gibraltar. Had Roderick known that he was going to be arrested on the high seas?

Magistrate Pizzarello confirmed that he had been approached for the warrant after Newall had been intercepted and was already on his way to the colony. Attorney-General Gittings submitted that whether Newall had intended to go to Gibraltar or the Canaries was irrelevant, adding that he was 'lawfully arrested at sea on a British vessel'.

But Finch confidently fought back, claiming that Newall had been asked to board HMS *Argonaut* on the pretence of having to show his papers and was then returned to Gibraltar at gunpoint. 'This has all the characteristics of an unlawful arrest,' continued Finch. 'We must consider why they went through all this trickery and coercion. This is the closest to modern piracy that one can imagine.' He went on to quote from the crime involving the train robber, Ronnie Biggs, and asked Pizzarello, 'Are we to become the extradition box of the world?'

But Gittings felt that Finch's submissions were naïve and pointed out that the police had been searching for an alleged double murderer. 'This man was wanted for two murders in which no bodies were found,' he continued, 'and we do not know the circumstances. Mr and Mrs Newall came to a violent end; it could have been a knife or a gun. What were the officers expected to do? Are we to say – "Would you mind popping over for a moment, we want to arrest you for murdering your mother and father?"' He continued by pointing out that the naval vessels had done what they were entitled to do and added that the judge's concern began only when the vessel entered

Gibraltar waters. As to the operation being planned and far from accidental, Gittings stated, 'The law is clear and has been since Dr Crippen was arrested in New York in around 1913. The man was lawfully arrested on the high seas for double murder. Your jurisdiction starts here. Whether he was arrested at gunpoint or imprisoned upside down, he arrived here in one piece and not injured. He faces charges of patricide and matricide.'

As a result Roderick did what he had done at La Moye and went on a hunger strike. His shock at being arrested when he had hoped to have got clear away and his subsequent acute depression might have been responsible for this – or it could have been a desire to protract events in court for as long as possible. He was also complaining of inhumane treatment at the Moorish Castle prison and, day by day, his desperation must have been increasing.

At the next hearing details emerged concerning the kind of melodramatic bravado Roderick could demonstrate – this instance by telling MacDowall that he had thought of trying to escape but had calculated on being hit by four bullets before he could grab a gun. It was an unfortunate statement in the circumstances which established a James Bond image for the tabloids. It also gave Gittings the opportunity to describe Roderick as a dangerous man, adding that if he was released he would be likely to use his fortune to escape to a safe place. Although all this was naturally hotly denied by Finch, Gittings continued to score useful points, adding that Newall had used his military training and anti-surveillance techniques to make a getaway from Britain. The very worst image that Roderick could possibly have projected at this crucial time was the tough, ruthless, military-trained, international desperado who would take every means at his disposal to evade justice.

Pizzarello ruled against Finch's submission that the warrant had not been properly obtained and the arrest at sea was illegal, and as a result refused his application to release Newall. The magistrate went on to state that he would not even consider bail until he had seen more evidence. Finch then claimed Newall was entitled to bail and had asked him to raise several points. The crux of the defence's argument was the validity of the Jersey warrant – for Roderick claimed he had never absconded from the island. Indeed, he had lived in the Falklands, another British colony, during a period of some four years and by being detained on Gibraltar he was prevented from running his charter business based there, having already put a lot of work into it. The business would soon be at risk and he would be deprived of the wherewithal to run his affairs.

Finch then went on to allege that Newall had been followed in Britain and allowed to leave. Moreover, in effecting his arrest unnecessary brutality had been used. 'There had been no need to tie his hands with electrical cable and handcuffs and hold him like this for eleven hours.'

Gittings intervened to say that the manner of arrest was not germane to a bail application. He stated, 'We all learnt at our mother's knee that there are only three issues which have to be addressed: if he [the defendant] will turn up, if he will interfere with other witnesses and if he will commit a further offence.'

Undaunted, Finch pointed out that his client's treatment in prison had not been a happy experience. His catalogue of complaints included the fact that Newall had not been moved to better cells but was being kept virtually in solitary confinement. He was told the authorities had been instructed to keep him as a high security prisoner. Finch also alleged that telephone conversations were being listened to. 'After one call to me he was told not to tell me what conditions in prison are like. It is an outrage and a disgrace.'

Finch went on to state that the *Austral Soma*, worth some £350,000, was not being properly looked after. Provisions had been left rotting and he (the counsel) had not been given a proper inventory. Newall, Finch continued, was being refused newspapers, and he asked the court to intervene, saying that human rights and dignity were at stake. 'He had only just received a copy of his Filofax to contact friends.' Finch added dismissively, 'Jersey has not heard of the fax machine. As a result of this treatment, last Sunday Mr Newall refused to take solid food. That position is likely to continue until he receives fair and right treatment.'

Finch hoped that the judge would take into account the facts that Newall had been at liberty for some years and that the yacht could be used as security. 'This person needs an opportunity to put his affairs in order. Also a reasonable opportunity to discuss his case with his counsel free from prying eyes and ears.' He went on to say that bail could be granted even if it included a provision that Newall be kept in a secure place in Gibraltar.

In what was a conclusion to an angry exchange between himself and Finch, Gittings then listed counsel's arguments and ended by saying that it had all been 'good lineage, but nothing to do with your [the magistrate's] serious responsibility'.

The Attorney-General stated that for a thousand years, ever since the days of sheriffs in Nottingham, the police had arrested whom they wanted and just put them in prison, but in 1958 people became entitled to bail. However, he said, while one could take this for granted if someone stole a Mars bar, 'double murder is different'. Such a person, if convicted, would face life imprisonment, probably with a recommendation that he should not be released for between twenty and twenty-five years. If a person were facing twenty years for murder in a Victorian prison in England, there would be a strong inducement for him to abscond, he added, going on to describe Newall as a man who was 'happy to sail the world alone'.

'The seas of the South Atlantic hold no fears for him,' declared Gittings, adding that Newall had left the army in 1988 and had not reappeared until he visited his aunt's house in Fulham in July that year. 'He is trained in anti-surveillance and weaponry. He is a dangerous man.'

Gittings further stated that on 11th July Newall decided to visit his aunt, Nancy Clarke, and then went on to see his grandmother in North Berwick. Following this he went to see his father's twin brother, Stephen Newall, and his wife Gaye at the Dunkeld House Hotel in Perthshire.

'During a three to four-hour conversation with Stephen Newall and Auntie Gaye he made statements amounting to an admission that he had killed his mother and father,' said Gittings, adding that the court would see statements to this effect from Stephen and Gaye Newall.

'This is the most serious crime in the calendar. If allowed to go free he will abscond,' stated the Attorney-General, adding that when Newall evaded police surveillance on the M62 he had then gone off in a boat after leaving a letter for Emma Jane Lonsdale, which was sent by private post from Paris and posted in London, franked 6th August, when Newall had already left.

The note, said Gittings, read, 'See you in Brazil, but only time will tell.' In response to Finch's question as to what this meant, Gittings replied that it meant what it had to Mr Biggs – he would be difficult to get hold of.

Gittings pointed out that Newall might use his money

to aid escape and that his uncle and aunts might be in danger. The judge replied that if Newall knew that he was being followed, this put 'a complexion' on things. He said that at this stage he was refusing bail, but he would consider it once he had the evidence before him. Ordering the Attorney-General to look into Newall's treatment in prison he remanded him in custody for another week.

Roderick must have realised at this point that he stood little chance of gaining his freedom – even with such an innovative counsel. If Finch couldn't get him out of his Moorish jail, who could?

Shortly afterwards, Roderick was alleged to have smuggled a razor blade into his cell; certainly he slashed both his wrists and groin. He had been due in court that morning to hear further legal argument, but he was clearly so depressed that he couldn't face it; neither could he have had much confidence in the results.

But Roderick's self-mutilation was certainly no cry for help; according to official Gibraltar sources he was minutes away from losing his life when he was rushed to the intensive care unit of St Bernard's Hospital. A small amount of cocaine was also apparently found in his cell after he had been discovered hiding under the sheets by prison officers. Chris Finch made no comment in court about Roderick's suicide bid, but he did ask for the release of the *Austral Soma* which had been moored in the Royal Navy dockyard since Newall's arrest more than a month ago. It was agreed between Finch and Gittings that an application for the return of the yacht would be heard in chambers. In the meantime, the file of documents important to the extradition proceedings had arrived – a week ahead of schedule. This left the way clear for Pizzarello to arrange a date the following week for the extradition hearing to begin, although this would naturally depend on Roderick Newall's state of health.

By 11th September 1992, Roderick was making a 'good recovery' and his condition was described as 'stable', but the next blow to his hopes – if he had any left – was when Attorney-General Gittings refused to let Chris Finch have access to the tape the police made of Roderick's conversation with his uncle and aunt in Scotland. 'I don't have to produce anything I don't want to,' replied Gittings.

Roderick, looking pale and dressed as he had been on his five other appearances in a dark blazer and jeans, listened to this unpromising statement as he was remanded in custody yet again, and heard his counsel saying that he believed the extradition hearing would take five days.

The extradition procedure follows a very precise pattern. As HMS *Argonaut* entered Gibraltar harbour at midnight on Wednesday 7th August, an officer of the Gibraltar police told Roderick that he was being arrested by a provisional warrant issued under Section 6(1)(b) of the 1967 Fugitive Offenders Act.

The warrant had been signed by the colony's magistrate, Felix Pizzarello, and was based on information given by Detective Sergeant Eddie Yome of the Gibraltar police. Under the provisions of the Act, Judge Pizzarello immediately informed the colony's Governor, Admiral Sir Derek Reffell.

The next stage in the procedure was the making of a formal request for extradition by the Jersey authorities to those in Gibraltar. Because of the island's relationship with the British Government, this involved passing the request from the Attorney-General to the Bailiff, who sent it to the Lieutenant Governor. He then forwarded it to the

Home Office with a request that the Foreign and Commonwealth Office act on behalf of the island.

In order to fulfil the requirements of the Act, the request was accompanied by a warrant issued in Jersey for Newall's arrest and 'particulars of the person whose return is requested and of the facts upon which and the law under which he is accused . . . and evidence sufficient to justify the issue of a warrant for his arrest . . .'

The test of the sufficiency of the evidence is found elsewhere in the Act but extradition proceedings are not a trial to determine innocence or guilt. The onus on the prosecution is to produce to the magistrate sufficient evidence as would 'in the opinion of the Stipendiary Magistrate authorise the issue of a warrant' if the alleged offence had been committed in Gibraltar.

Once the Governor of Gibraltar received the request from Jersey he then made an order to the magistrate which is known as an 'authority to proceed'; without that order no proceedings for extradition can take place.

The Act then provides that once the 'authority to proceed' has been received by the magistrate, a hearing is fixed. If the magistrate is satisfied after hearing the evidence that it would be sufficient to warrant a trial had the alleged offence been committed in Gibraltar, then 'the court shall . . . commit him to custody to await his return thereunder'.

But that would not necessarily be the end of the Gibraltar proceedings, because under another section of the Fugitive Offenders Act, Newall could not be returned to Jersey for at least fifteen days.

The purpose of the delay is to enable a prisoner to apply to Gibraltar's Supreme Court for a writ of habeas corpus, a legal process which requires the detainee to be brought into court so that the lawfulness of the restraint may be investigated and determined.

A writ can be granted on three separate grounds, but the Jersey authorities believed that only one would be relevant in this particular case. It hung on the length of time between the disappearance of Nicholas and Elizabeth Newall in October 1987 and Roderick's arrest, and read, '. . . by reason of the passage of time since he is alleged to have committed [the offence] . . . it would, having regard to all the circumstances, be unjust or oppressive to return him'.

In the absence of a successful application for habeas corpus, the Governor had the power by warrant to order Newall's return, but he was not allowed to make the order if it appeared to him that it would be unjust or oppressive to return him.

Once the warrant had been issued, Newall could then be returned to Jersey.

Chris Finch decided to place the thrust of his defence case on the alleged conversation between Roderick and his uncle and aunt which the police had on tape and decided that amongst his witnesses he would call Stephen and Gaye Newall. The remainder would be two police officers. Roderick, in a private exchange with his lawyer, smiled for the first time in court. Limited optimism might be returning.

On 14th October 1992, Jersey's Attorney-General, Philip Bailhache, gave a last-minute instruction to the court, stating that no witnesses would be called and that the extradition request would 'rely on the tapes, authenticated witness statements and the transcripts'. Finch had put on considerable pressure to achieve this and the decision meant that the hearing could rapidly be brought forward.

On 22nd October, Roderick was once again refused bail and, during the session, there was a reference to the 'visitation' his aunt, Nancy Clarke, had received from her sister Elizabeth on the night she died and the fact that she had told Roderick about it when he saw her before his visit to Scotland that summer. Opposing Finch's bail application, Gittings said that Newall 'could disappear off the face of the earth . . . The Crown would say he would. He did. Six months after Mr and Mrs Newall disappeared, this young man left the army and disappeared almost from the face of the earth'. Gittings went on to challenge the viability of Newall's charter business in the Falklands. 'The money came from somewhere. Maybe it came from his uncle [Kenneth Newall of Sark] who coincidentally died four weeks after Mr and Mrs Newall.'

At once, Chris Finch accused the Attorney-General of 'vilifying the accused' and making claims he could not justify. He also criticised the 'high level of weaponry' being used by the police, stating that it was not welcome by the people of Gibraltar. Pizzarello refused bail, saying that he would do so at least until he had heard the tape recording.

Gittings stated that the tape would be given to the judge and defence counsel 'in days'. Roderick then stood up and asked, 'How many? Weeks? Months?'

But by 27th October, the tapes had arrived and Finch told Pizzarello that he had no objection to him listening to them in his chambers. Newall was remanded yet again. Gittings stated that the tapes ran for four and a half hours and the Crown alleged that this included a half-hour interval when Roderick went for a walk with his aunt.

Finch then told Pizzarello, 'I ask you to listen very carefully, see if you detect one word where he says what he is alleged to have said.'

By 18th November, Chris Finch was saying that the

'over-reporting, comment and speculation' would 'clearly prejudice' a future trial in Jersey and that legal argument over the admissibility of the alleged tape-recorded 'confession' should be held in camera. He also added that since Pizzarello had now heard the tapes he would appreciate the numerous references to third parties who were neither in court nor represented there. Finch stated that it was not practice for third parties in suspect crimes to be named and said that there were three or four in this case. Finally, he commented, 'It will be difficult for me to discharge my duty fully if every word is published far and wide.'

Pizzarello replied that submissions on the matter would be heard when the hearing opened the next morning.

Meanwhile security precautions were unprecedented, mainly because of a rumour that was sweeping Gibraltar to the effect that a possible attempt might be made to 'spring' Roderick from jail. Who would do this was difficult to say, but it was just more fuel to his gathering reputation as some kind of international conspirator. Nothing could have been further from the truth.

On Saturday, 21st November, Roderick received good news – that the tape recording on which he was alleged to have confessed to his uncle and aunt that he had murdered his parents could not be used as evidence in his extradition. His relief, however, was limited as Chris Finch must have told him that this would not give him his freedom.

In ruling the tapes 'inadmissible as evidence', Pizzarello said that Newall had not made a specific admission to murder. This raised the interesting point that Roderick had possibly not referred at all to the actual murder of his parents but only to the disposal of their bodies.

Pizzarello made every effort to see the issue in as clear

a light as possible. The wording of his ruling shows the extent of his conscientious impartiality.

When he heard the tape, three points occurred to him. Firstly, the defendant had made no admission to murder. Secondly, the defendant had disposed of or aided and abetted the disposal of the bodies. Thirdly, Roderick, in the words of de Silva (Desmond de Silva, the London QC representing the Crown), 'indulged in a verbal ballet led by uncle and aunt'.

Pizzarello stated, 'It seemed to me to be right to indicate to counsel that if the tapes were admitted it would not be difficult, subject to hearing argument, to infer that only an assassin or an aider or abettor or an accessory after the fact would have dealt with the bodies in the manner alleged, and there was then a prima facie case to answer.'

He went on to point out that the prosecution sought to lead the tapes in evidence on the grounds that the admissions, such as they were, were made voluntarily.

'Counsel went into some detail as to why the prosecution said that the statements were voluntary and sought to seek that they had in no way been obtained through oppression. He submitted that there was no prejudice held out to him by a person in authority, that there was no hope of advantage held out by a person in authority that was temporal in nature, there was no oppression that sapped his free will, any exhortation being of a moral kind.'

Pizzarello said that Roderick Newall had gone to the meeting with his uncle and aunt voluntarily. No one had coerced him to take up his uncle's invitation to meet him at the hotel and he need not have gone. He also entered into conversation freely.

De Silva had made the point that at that stage the police had not sufficient evidence to caution Roderick, but there was nothing legally in the Judge's Rules to condemn this technically and the evidence was therefore admissible. He also submitted that even if the Rules were against such an interview, the court had a discretion 'which he asked me in the circumstances of the case to exercise in favour of doing it'.

Pizzarello said that although the defendant was unaware of the secret tape recording, the Crown case was that it did 'not render the admission any less voluntary'. De Silva had also submitted that the fact that the uncle and aunt knew of the recording made no difference either. 'They were, to an extent, an extension of the police but they were not persons in authority.'

The defence position put by Chris Finch, shorn of its emotional content, was simply that Roderick Newall was under suspicion, and therefore if the police wished to question him they should have cautioned him before the interview with his uncle and aunt. Instead, the police had arranged with Stephen and Gaye Newall that they should bring up 'certain matters', and Pizzarello mentioned the deposition of Stephen Newall to substantiate that.

'He [Chris Finch] submits that [the] uncle and aunt are an extension of the police and the defendant was inveigled into making admissions which he would not otherwise have made. In any case he says that the admissions made do not point to his being the murderer; they were consistent with the defendant's attempt to cover up for another.'

Pizzarello went on to say that Finch had stated that the first part of the interview was innocuous and the parents' death was not brought up by Roderick but by his uncle. But the main point was, how could he be said to have come to his uncle to unburden himself of his guilt? Chris Finch stated that the defendant appeared to have broken down, and submitted that the questioning of Roderick Newall, however delicately put, in those circumstances clearly sapped his free will. Also some hope was held out to the defendant by his uncle when there was discussion concerning a short prison sentence and 'the uncle's wish to put a full stop on all this'.

Pizzarello added that Finch further submitted that 'the uncle's and aunt's words, honeyed as they were, were despicable in that they were deliberately calculated to lead to an unwary admission, that much of what was said was all lies on the part of the uncle and aunt, that it was all a front for the police to obtain their evidence. It was all part of a huge fraud, a conspiracy by the police and uncle to get what they could not otherwise if the defendant's right to silence had been honoured.'

In those circumstances, said Pizzarello, Finch had submitted that the confession was inadmissible. The prosecution, he stated, had not proved beyond reasonable doubt that the admission/confession was obtained voluntarily and that the content of the tapes was capable of a different interpretation.

'I must say that when I heard the tapes it seemed to me that the uncle and aunt were genuinely concerned about (a) what had happened to the defendant's mother and father; (b) where the bodies were; (c) to give such support as they could to the defendant; (d) to give help to the police.'

Pizzarello stated that none of these concerns were mutually exclusive and, although one might be more forceful than another, in the absence of hearing Stephen Newall and Gaye Newall it was his opinion that he ought to view 'the preponderant motive as helping the police which, after all, is what any member of the public is enjoined to do'.

But Pizzarello didn't forget that another consideration was the decision to bring the defendant to justice, the uncle being a brother of the murdered man.

He went on to say, 'Mr Finch railed at the unfairness of the police practice in this case. How the whole affair was stage-managed with lies and deceit against the defendant. I would pause to point out that if the police suspicions were correct they were dealing with a murderer against whom there was no hard evidence, and I think that in their investigative process they are surely entitled to use as many stratagems as they can in order to secure evidence.

'If, hypothetically, Roderick Newall had said where the bodies were, because he knew where they were, vital evidence might be forthcoming from the scene of the burial which, if it involved him, would certainly be, in my opinion, good admissible evidence against him notwithstanding that the present interview were inadmissible.

'As for uncle and aunt, while treachery, lies and deceit might be the perception of the defendant and those advising him, another view of the matter is that they were very brave people to have – in the belief that they were dealing with a murderer – been in his company in the room at the hotel and gone for a walk, albeit that police presence was close by. That is how it struck me, although I understand from Mr Finch's interjection that the defendant's uncle's status is such that a situation of this kind can be met by him without undue fluster.'

Pizzarello stated that the admissibility of the tapes could be said to depend on whether they could be regarded as a voluntary confession or not. However, in fact, if there was no confession involved, the evidence on the tape would be admissible and could be put to the jury for a decision. Also, if the contents of the tape were not a confession they would be sufficient to raise a prima facie case for the defendant to answer – on which the court would be bound to commit.

'In my view,' he continued, 'the tape is put forward by

the prosecution as a confession or at any rate statements prejudicial to the defendant which amount to a confession; and, having read it, it is on this basis that I approach the submissions. It seems to me . . . the conversations entered into by the defendant and his uncle and aunt were quite voluntary.' Pizzarello continued by saying that if the tape *was* a trap, he was quite unaware of it, 'and the fact that he was entrapped does not go to the root of voluntariness.'

Pizzarello agreed with de Silva that there was not enough evidence to caution Roderick Newall and 'there is a grey area where the police, on investigating a case, become suspicious . . . and then get hard fact.' He accepted Finch's contention that the police had reasonable suspicion, 'but it was of a kind where they had their hands tied and they could not progress further unless they had the co-operation of the defendant.'

He added however that the police needed the information. 'It might have been that if the police had construed the conversations in the manner that Mr Finch submits (which is essentially a matter for a jury), there would have been no subsequent proceedings; but this was not and is not the view of the police.

'However, not until the interview was over could the police be said to have sufficient evidence of that, because – and I think this is very important – any connection by the defendant with the murder is only a matter of inference from the conversation in which the defendant did not admit the murder and where he gives information which may be detrimental to his position.'

This information, Pizzarello stated, was in response to 'the loaded and leading questions gently put by his uncle, and I may say the uncle did not put anything difficult to him.'

Pizzarello stated that de Silva submitted that, although Stephen and Gaye Newall were acting as extensions of the police, that was no reason why the evidence obtained on the tape should be excluded.

'He refers to *Jelen v. Katz* which he submits can properly be cited even though it is a post-PACE [Police and Criminal Evidence Act] case. This case went beyond deliberate over-hearing of a defendant in conversation: the witness accused the defendant.

'There was an element of entrapment, the Court of Appeal said. But did that make it unfair so as to require the judge in the exercise of his discretion to exclude the evidence? He took the view that it was not unfair, and we can see no reason to disagree with him.'

Pizzarello said that the circumstances of each case were different and it was relevant to point out that the tape recording could be admitted in evidence unless the conversation was unfairly conducted by the witness.

Pizzarello felt that the tape recording had to be treated in the nature of a confession. 'It is prima facie receivable in evidence but in the exercise of my discretion and in the circumstances of this case, I disallow it. It is unfair to the defendant.

'More importantly, it was brought into being by the calculated act of the police through the agency of persons who could lull the defendant into a false sense of security (note the remark that he would go to his uncle for advice). I do not believe the police acted improperly in the investigative sense, but it is clearly improper in the forensic sense, for they used an avenue "in a sneaky way" of circumventing the right to silence.'

Pizzarello once again proved to be both liberal and fair-minded, and his conscientious approach and considered judgment gave hope to Finch and Newall.

*   *   *

By 25th November, the Crown had rallied, causing Chris Finch to claim they had acted like 'thieves in the night' when he was not represented as they applied for a judicial review of Pizzarello's decision not to allow the tapes as evidence. Finch said, 'This is a sad episode in a litany of sad episodes affecting this case.' During the delay, Roderick Newall was still not allowed bail. Nevertheless, despite the attempt to overturn Pizzarello's judgment, Roderick must have been once again reasonably hopeful until the police suddenly moved against him with new evidence; the prosecution disclosed that they had a new affidavit which was 'significant' in implicating Newall in the death of his parents.

On 17th December, Chief Justice Alistair Kneller overturned the ruling made by Pizzarello, stating that he had exercised a discretion he did not have. The defence, now reinforced with Brian Leavy QC, a senior barrister of London's Middle Temple, immediately gave notice of Kneller's decision to the Gibraltar Court of Appeal – which was not due to sit until 8th March 1993. Next day, the mystery witness was flown into Jersey from Brazil. She was Elena Pedo. Roderick must have been aghast at this apparent betrayal. His admissions to her, so many thousands of miles away, had perhaps seemed only a voice in the wilderness, and it is unlikely that he had bargained on the Jersey police's initiative in leafing through his Filofax. Nor had he anticipated Elena Pedo's apparent satisfaction at stepping into the limelight.

Marks and Adamson had secretly flown to the Sao Paulo Consulate only to find that Elena had changed her mind and didn't want to talk to the two officers after all and was refusing to emerge from Porto Legre which was a two-hour flight away. They were met by the British Consul whom Marks remembers as a 'guy in [a] white suit, looking every inch the British gent.'

Eventually Elena agreed to come to their hotel and Marks and Adamson took her out to dinner. She refused wine as well as refusing to talk, at this stage, about her relationship with Roderick. The officers returned to London but days later Elena Pedo was flown in to Heathrow.

Marks remembers that she was 'ages coming off the plane. We were at the door of the plane [as] she'd never been abroad before. We looked after her, took her to the hotel, did all that. We flew down to Jersey, on the same flight but ignoring each other. Somebody whipped her straight away. She didn't go anywhere near Police Head-quarters. She was picked up by a woman detective. She only had a quick whizz round the island, in terms of sight-seeing, and then straight to the Bailiff's house.'

Marks had received information that when he was arrested Roderick had been heading for Brazil and for Elena, with a possible intention of marrying her and 'doing a Ronnie Biggs'.

'Whether that was to bolt or not I don't really know because I don't think he realised what he'd done in Scotland,' Marks recalled. 'The secrecy about the fact that we had a warrant for his arrest was being maintained, with the co-operation of the media, but it wasn't going to stay a secret for long. It was only a question of who told him first. But he was definitely expected in Brazil.'

Elena Pedo, now considerably frightened, was not likely to want to be a 'Mrs Biggs'.

10

Chris Finch immediately set about preparing a request to interview Elena himself. Earlier, she had been interviewed at length at her home in Brazil by Detective Inspector Jim Adamson before being flown to London and then to Jersey, where she swore an affidavit before Sir Peter Crill. Ironically, and possibly to Crill's amazement, she took a photograph of the signing ceremony in his house which she may have felt she could sell to the press on her return to Brazil. Elena Pedo, camera at the ready, was clearly determined not to miss out on the drama, but also to preserve it for posterity.

Meanwhile, back at the Moorish Castle prison, Roderick heard the disappointing news that his lawyers were not to be allowed a meeting with Elena Pedo and that Attorney-General Philip Bailhache QC had said, 'In the light of the nature of the evidence given by Miss Pedo, it seems to me to be an extraordinary request and it's a request which will be refused as far as I'm concerned.'

Clearly, Elena's affidavit must have involved Roderick's confession to her after the cinema in Miami. The frustrating response was too much to bear, and on 23rd December he made a second suicide attempt and was rushed once again to St Bernard's Hospital where he was said to be 'unconscious and having fits'. He remained in the intensive care unit for three days, having apparently taken either an overdose of pills given to him as part of his daily medication, or drugs that may have been smuggled in to him. Unfortunately the smuggling of drugs into British prisons is becoming commonplace, providing the recipient can pay the going rate. Shortly after his admission to hospital he was stomach-pumped and an enquiry into his suicide attempt was launched by the Gibraltar police. He regained consciousness late on Christmas Day.

By 31st December, Chris Finch was complaining that Roderick was being 'frozen to death' by the prison authorities and strip-searched three times a day. He also told two lay magistrates that his client had not made a second suicide bid, and stated that the overdose which had put Roderick Newall in a coma for three days was caused by barbiturates mainly supplied by the prison authorities themselves.

Gittings said that he would look into the claims, but this did not mean that he accepted the conditions were as Finch had alleged. He continued, 'Since 5 August the defendant, of his own volition, had been on a self-imposed hunger strike. He attempted suicide by lacerating his body, which, I was told by doctors, took him to minutes from death at his own will.'

Gittings went on to refer to the recent overdose but Chris Finch interrupted him, stating that none of this was relevant to the complaint that Newall was being kept in a cold cell with no proper clothing. Gittings replied that Newall was being searched regularly and was in a cell isolated from other people. 'If he had not attempted suicide twice . . .' he continued. Roderick then intervened by stamping his feet loudly.

Finch immediately declared that 'it was not established that this was a second suicide attempt'. He went on to add that he had complained continuously of poor conditions which 'could lead to desperate measures'. Stating that Roderick was being kept in a pair of shorts, Finch added, 'It may be that segregation and monitoring is necessary, but not this.' The magistrate then recommended that conditions should be 'as good as security and reasonableness allow', and remanded Roderick Newall in custody until 8th January.

In fact conditions at the Moorish Castle prison were by no means as barbaric as Chris Finch implied. The prison was equipped with a pool room, mini-gym and table tennis facilities and the prisoners had access to television and radio as well as national and local newspapers. Roderick, being on remand, would also have been able to receive visitors and write as many letters as he wished. However, he was segregated because of his suicide attempts, and would have spent twenty-three hours a day in his cell with only one hour being set aside for exercise.

By 8th January, Finch was accusing the Jersey authorities of 'deliberately leaking' confidential information to the *Jersey Evening Post*. This complaint referred to a piece published on 21st December and concerned the request made by Finch to interview Elena Pedo – the request that was turned down by Jersey's Attorney-General. Mike Bisson, the editor of the newspaper, denied the source of the information was in Jersey and stated, 'As we reported in the article of 21 December, the information was obtained from legal sources in the colony. I am not prepared to disclose the identity of our informant but can categorically state that it was neither someone in Jersey nor someone from Jersey in Gibraltar in connection with the case.'

Finch considered the leak 'highly prejudicial and unfair to Mr Newall'.

The Appeal Court was due to sit towards the end of March, but on the 17th the police came up with another shock for Roderick. They had arrested Mark in Paris for the alleged murder of his parents.

The arrest may well have been an attempt by the police to put even more pressure on the Newall brothers. Mark was detained at 9 a.m. by officers of the French Brigade Criminelle and an application to extradite him from France was made by Bailhache. The Jersey police stated that Mark Stephen Nelson Newall (26) was arrested on a warrant that was issued at 5 p.m. the previous Friday, 12th March, by the Bailiff, Sir Peter Crill, 'for the offence of murdering Nicholas Newall and Elizabeth Newall, née Nelson, on or about 10th October, 1987'.

He was ordered to be detained in Paris's main remand prison, La Santé, until a formal application for extradition was received. Under the provisions of the Council of Europe Treaty No. 24, the Jersey authorities had sixteen days in which to inform their French colleagues of the facts of the case. It appeared that the extradition would be a fairly simple matter.

Roderick responded by trying to kill himself again, this time using a syringe that was thought to have been brought into the prison inside an orange. Mark's arrest must have been the appalling shock to his conscience that the police may well have predicted.

On 18th March, with Roderick once again recovered and remanded, pending his appearance before the colony's Court of Appeal the following week, Chris Finch drove across the border to Malaga in Spain to catch a flight to

Paris where he was to attempt to see Mark. The *Jersey Evening Post* reported, 'Mark Newall is at present being held in Paris's main remand prison, La Santé, and the legal position regarding contact with visitors is not known, although it is understood that the Jersey authorities may well be considering expressing objections to their French colleagues if Mr Finch tries to see his client's brother.'

On Tuesday, 23rd March, the Court of Appeal dismissed Roderick Newall's appeal against a ruling by the colony's Chief Justice, Alistair Kneller, that Magistrate Felix Pizzarello was wrong to disallow the tapes from the extradition proceedings he was hearing. The written judgment was expected within two or three weeks and Finch announced that he wanted a further three weeks after its delivery to consider a possible appeal to the Privy Council.

De Silva, appearing for the Crown, described Elena Pedo's statement as a 'confession by this defendant to the fact that he had murdered his parents'. He also asked for costs – estimated at £80,000 – and Finch replied that this would be an 'intolerable burden' for his client. The court agreed, rejecting the application.

Roderick, smartly dressed in a blazer, blue shirt and the regimental tie of the Royal Green Jackets, looked every inch the cool young subaltern, despite all his physical suffering; inwardly he must have been reeling from the continuous onslaught of shockwaves. Mark's arrest, and what Roderick may have seen as Elena's betrayal, and the rejection of the tape appeal had made him realise that he was only playing a waiting game and that extradition was closing in on him fast. He was running out of all options – except the increasingly familiar one of ending his own life.

On 12th April, with the help of a small modelling knife, Roderick Newall slashed his wrists again, but he survived the attempt with only minor injuries and did not need hospitalisation. However, because blood poisoning set in, he was given yet another week's remand – and at this point may well have wondered if he could continue to spend the rest of his life in the prison. His lawyer, Chris Finch, ducked and weaved, and never let an opportunity pass for another legal avenue to be explored.

By 21st April, Roderick had written a letter to his lawyers stating that if he went on hunger strike again he did not want to be force-fed or to receive medical attention.

Meanwhile, Mark was stating that he was quite willing to return to Jersey on a voluntary basis, despite the fact that he was still awaiting extradition procedures, and he eventually arrived back in Jersey on the afternoon of 30th April 1993, in a specially chartered jet from Le Bourget.

Assistant Chief Officer Marks remembers his first sighting of the apartment where the French police had already arrested Mark. 'He was sitting on a chair, handcuffed . . . and looking a bit pale and surprised. The warrant allowed us to search the place from top to bottom . . . it was rather a splendid place – on two levels.' There was a mirrored salon, with a couple of imitation trees, a spiral staircase leading up to two en-suite bedrooms and a small roof garden. At first, Mark Newall appeared to have confused Paul Marks with a diplomat looking after his interests. When he told Newall that he was a police officer Mark replied that he had not met him before and assumed he had come from London. Paul Marks recalled, 'I said no. I came from Jersey. It was the Jersey police which, I think, he felt were not up to it.'

When Mark Newall was taken to the Judge's Chambers that night he immediately said, 'Tell the Bailiff I'm willing to come back. I don't want to stay here.' He was as cool and as calm as ever. At the airport, a martial arts expert stood by in case Mark became violent. He closed his eyes on the plane as it took off from Paris and did not reopen them until he arrived in Jersey. That evening he was charged with murder. After being cautioned Mark said, 'I have no statement to make at this time, other than I'm not guilty of the offences that I'm charged with.' This was to be the most testing time for Mark Newall's iron-clad nerves. He spent the night in the cells in the Rouge Bouillon police station. On 1st May, he was transferred to La Moye prison.

On the morning of Tuesday, 4th May, Mark pleaded not guilty to murdering his parents when he appeared at the police court. He was charged 'with Roderick Innes Nelson Newall', his elder brother, who was still being held in Gibraltar, with murdering Nicholas Park Newall and Elizabeth Newall, née Nelson, on or about 10th October 1987.

He stood impassively during the one-minute hearing, wearing a smart dark grey suit, light blue shirt and a blue patterned tie, looking across the court room through round gold-rimmed spectacles. The streets around the court had been cordoned off; only the press were allowed into the area. Mark was accompanied by Advocate Ashley Hoy and barrister Peter Barnes, son of Angela Barnes, an executor, along with Mark and Roderick, of the missing couple's wills.

The following statement was issued that morning by the office of Advocate David Le Quesne. Paris counsel Anthony van Hagen, acting on behalf of Mark Newall, said, 'Mr Newall has never been, at any time, a fugitive from the Jersey police authorities and has always voluntarily assisted the police with their enquiries. Mr Newall has made numerous visits to both Jersey and the UK since the disappearance of his parents and, following his brother's arrest, the Jersey police categorically informed him that they had no intention of questioning him any further. As Mr Newall voluntarily kept the Jersey police informed of his whereabouts in the event that his assistance might be required, he was shocked and distressed to be arrested and an extradition request made by authorities [to] whom he has always given full co-operation in the past. My office was instructed by Mr Newall not to resist the extradition, but to facilitate and speed up the extradition process, as our client wished to return to Jersey immediately to respond to any allegations made against him. Mr Newall has instructed Jersey counsel and will defend the allegations against him.'

Meanwhile, Stephen Newall and Nancy Clarke were now determined to inherit the Newall estate – and to wrest it away from Mark and Roderick. Although presumably some of the money had been spent – particularly in relation to Roderick's Falklands charter business – there must have been a considerable sum remaining. This action, of course, was only proposed if the brothers were found guilty of murdering their parents.

Both Stephen Newall and Nan Clarke were now asking the Royal Court to order that they replace Roderick and Mark as beneficiaries of the estate of Nicholas and Elizabeth.

A statement was then issued from Mark's solicitors. It read, 'Roderick and Mark Newall are innocent of any crime concerning their parents unless and until they have been convicted of such crime. Even if Roderick and Mark Newall were liable upon conviction to the forfeiture of inherited assets [as a matter of law this is very doubtful] the actions now being taken by their uncle and aunt over these assets must seem greedy and distasteful. At a time when Roderick and Mark are vulnerable and isolated and in need of support from family and friends, this action by their uncle and aunt is a cruel blow.'

An immediate interim injunction preventing the brothers from selling a house that was part of the estate of Nicholas and Elizabeth Newall was already in place.

The application was adjourned *sine die* in the Royal Court on 21st May and both parties agreed to appear at forty-eight hours' notice.

Roderick over a long period, and Mark over a far shorter one, were no doubt finding that all these legal bursts of activity, however stressful, at least filled some of the long, lonely hours of waiting.

The authorities in Gibraltar now considered that Roderick could join Mark in Jersey in just a couple of months' time and the *Jersey Evening Post* reported on 27th May 1993, 'The former soldier, arrested on the high seas last August, may be considering accepting formal extradition from Gibraltar without a full hearing, according to defence lawyer, Chris Finch.'

Roderick's extradition hearing had been arranged for 19th July and had originally been set for five days, but Finch was now saying that it could be held sooner – any afternoon at short notice – and might then last just half a day. Roderick must have been almost broken. Did he now want to return to Jersey and confess? Was he too weary to continue the fight? It was of course likely that he wanted to try and protect his brother who was now facing a double murder charge. In any case, the formal hearing would include the now admissible taped evidence so it certainly did not seem worth holding out any longer. The end of the tactical game was at last in sight.

11

As Finch had been occupying the high ground about the alleged poor prison conditions for so long, Gittings reminded the court at the next remand hearing that the reason for Roderick Newall's isolation was to protect him as a result of four apparent suicide attempts. The judge however responded, 'How much of those disturbing incidents are the results of conditions?' He asked the Attorney-General to bear that point in mind.

On 18th June Roderick broke his near-silence in court to express his frustration at being kept in solitary confinement. His lawyer, Chris Finch, made the point yet again that this isolation could lead to anxiety, self-mutilation or suicide. He added that Roderick Newall was not being treated like a human being and was 'trussed up like a chicken' when he was originally brought to the prison and was still subjected to a daily strip search. Finch went on to warn that international organisations would come to investigate Gibraltar's prison conditions when they heard of Roderick's situation.

Gittings argued back that Newall played chess, Scrabble and dominoes with prison staff, watched Sky television and was in constant contact with other people. He also claimed the Moorish Castle prison was civilised compared with Wandsworth or Pentonville in the UK. Finch simply retaliated by stating that the Gibraltar authorities were ignoring his repeated calls for improvements in conditions for his client.

Gittings returned with an example of the reasoning behind Roderick's current solitary confinement. He referred to an incident when he had allegedly claimed that he could get anything he wanted into the prison. He had asked a guard if a book he had been given in prison had been checked, then produced a blade from the spine of the book 'with a smile'. Roderick then told the court, 'But I handed it in and one time before as well.' He sounded like a naughty boy caught out by the prefects and was once again suffering from a mixture of attempted superiority and bravado.

Answering suggestions that other cell mates could provide him with such items, Roderick said, 'I have not had contact with mates for six months.'

Finch then pointed out that Mark Newall, now at La Moye prison in Jersey, worked in the kitchens and mixed with other prisoners. Gittings replied that Mark had not been on a hunger strike, had not been found with oranges with syringes in them and had not attempted suicide four times. With regard to television viewing, however, Gittings had to admit that the video was 'on the blink'.

Then, just when it seemed that events in the Gibraltar courts were rapidly running out of steam, the situation abruptly changed.

When Mark Newall appeared in the police court in Jersey on 5th July, defence counsel Advocate David Le Quesne stated that a Law Lords decision reported only the previous week could vitally affect the question of Roderick Newall's extradition.

Counsel stated that the case, *R. v. Horseferry Road Magistrates' Court (ex-parte Bennett)*, empowered the High Court to investigate the circumstances in extradition procedures as to how a defendant came to be brought to a jurisdiction.

Advocate Le Quesne pointed out that in the light of the Law Lords decision, Roderick Newall could now make an application to the Gibraltar Supreme Court.

Le Quesne continued, 'He was hijacked on his boat on the open seas and Mr Finch, the counsel in Gibraltar, is trying to get the full report of the case reported last week and will be relying on that authority before the Supreme Court.

'It will take about six weeks at the earliest, to bring that matter before the Supreme Court, so it is even more highly unlikely that Roderick Newall will be brought back to Jersey this year, if at all.'

In repeating the arguments made the previous week, counsel stated that the Crown had a prima facie case against Mark Newall, but was, in effect, not yet prepared to bring it before the court.

Jersey police court Assistant Magistrate David Trott asked, 'How do I know that they have a prima facie case?'

Counsel replied, 'Exactly, sir. You do not know until they put the evidence before you.'

As a result of this new move – and possible last-ditch loophole for Roderick – Mark was to discover in eight days whether Assistant Magistrate Trott was prepared to instruct the Crown to order that committal proceedings against him should go ahead independently of Roderick being returned from Gibraltar. For a change the heat was on Mark. Was Roderick, after all, going to get away with the murder of his parents, in which case had an arrangement or agreement been reached between the prosecution and the defence? This might possibly have said that, unless evidence was found after Roderick returned to Jersey which could implicate Mark in the deaths of his parents, the murder charges against him would be dropped.

In mid-July Chris Finch filed papers with the Supreme Court asking for a date to be set for the end of August to 'hear arguments over how the former Royal Green Jackets officer was brought to Gibraltar'.

A few days later Roderick's lawyers were expected to apply for a writ of habeas corpus. The application was to be contested by Jersey's Attorney-General, Philip Bailhache QC, and could begin a lengthy legal process which might reach the Privy Council. It was also established that in any case the writ was unlikely to be heard before Gibraltar's Supreme Court until September.

This delay was caused by prosecution opposition and further attempts to persuade Pizzarello to hear the extradition proceedings before the defence's application was known. He refused, and Crown lawyers then went to the Supreme Court for a writ which would order Pizzarello to hear the extradition.

These fresh complexities gave Roderick Newall his final spark of hope. No doubt his fervour fanned the spark into a flame.

At the beginning of August, Lord Merivale, an RAF hero who was mentioned in despatches in the Second World War, took up Roderick's case as a member of the House of Lords, pointing out that he had been incarcerated for far too long. He wrote to the Foreign and Commonwealth Offices enquiring not only about the length of time Roderick had been in custody but also about the conditions at the Moorish Castle prison where he had made his four suicide bids.

The Southern European Department of the Foreign Office replied, pointing out that Newall's defence counsel, Chris Finch, had opposed every attempt by the Jersey and Gibraltar authorities to extradite Newall from Gibraltar. Meanwhile, efforts continued in Jersey for independent committal proceedings for Mark Newall.

On 20th August 1993, the Supreme Court in Gibraltar rejected the application to investigate the allegedly illegal circumstances surrounding Roderick's arrest until after extradition proceedings were completed. Chris Finch had called his last shot on Roderick's behalf – and lost. 'Why bother with constitutional law,' remarked Finch, 'if you can just send out a gunboat and bring him in?' Extradition proceedings were to begin on 8th September, but there were to be more delays.

The *Jersey Evening Post* reported that 'An extradition hearing is due to take place in the colony's magistrates' court in September, but Roderick's lawyers say that the legal process is far from complete and if he is to be extradited it will be many months before he is brought back.'

Roderick, however, now knew that eventually he would have to return to Jersey, and although he could rely on Chris Finch for more attempts to prevent this he realised that in the end his confession was inevitable. There were no more suicide attempts; possibly he was now becoming reconciled to the inevitable. The spark of hope had gone but perhaps Roderick realised that it had only really existed in his own mind.

By 1st September, however, Finch declared that his client was anxious to use every legal process he could pursue in Gibraltar, as he believed that press coverage had already led to his having no possibility of a fair trial in Jersey.

Finch then won a delay of a month in the extradition hearing. This would now take place after 6th October, when the Gibraltar Court of Appeal would consider the habeas corpus application. At the last moment, Finch had scored again with his delaying tactics.

Patiently, fair-minded as ever, Pizzarello pointed out that while it might be difficult for that application to succeed, Newall might wish to apply, and as a result he would exercise his discretion and delay the extradition proceedings until after it had been heard.

Desmond de Silva QC, appearing for the Jersey authorities, gave notice immediately that he would seek a judicial review of Pizzarello's decision within the next few days, and so battle continued, each side taking up every tactic they could muster.

The legal fireworks were only damp squibs now, but nevertheless, Roderick Newall must have come to look on the liberal and perceptive Magistrate Pizzarello almost as an old friend – and certainly as a man of principle and integrity – and there is little doubt that he must have seen the innovative Chris Finch in much the same light.

The application for a writ of habeas corpus which would have tested the legality of Roderick's arrest was rejected by the Supreme Court in Gibraltar and at the end of September the Court of Appeal made it clear when they threw out his final appeal that they wanted the matter dealt with promptly.

The extradition proceedings could only go ahead by referring everything back to Pizzarello in the magistrates' court and this procedure was due to start on 6th October 1993. But Roderick's lawyers then stated that they wanted to bring a fresh application for legal aid. The court was told that the financial demands of the legal process involved in defending himself against extradition had bankrupted Newall. Pizzarello replied that he would have to provide affidavits to show that he was not the owner of the *Austral Soma* on which he was arrested.

Stuart Ross, who was an associate of Newall's counsel, Chris Finch, said the financial tap had been turned off and Gittings replied, estimating the *Austral Soma* to be worth approximately £350,000.

The extradition hearing formally resumed on Friday, 8th October 1993, when Desmond de Silva referred to statements made by Newall on the tape secretly made by the police during the conversation between Roderick and his uncle and aunt in Scotland. De Silva said these 'were an utter confession short of "did it myself"'. He referred to the killings having taken place on 10th October 1987, and told the magistrate, 'Five years later the accused gazed into the face of his father's identical twin. There then spilt from his lips the pent up guilt he had held for so long.' According to his Uncle Stephen, Roderick had told him and his wife that his parents' bodies were in plastic and camouflage and 'that the bodies had clothes on that would pin it down to the night'. De Silva stated that 'It is the case for the Crown that when these admissions are taken together with certain established events and scientific discoveries at the scene of the killing and elsewhere in Jersey, what emerges is a carefully planned and brutally executed double killing with infinite cunning being deployed in the disposal of the bodies that have never been found, and elaborate steps being taken to shield himself from the guilt which years later he confessed to.'

De Silva added that Stephen Newall said he hoped and prayed that Roderick would lead the authorities to the bodies so that they could have a decent burial. According

to the same sources, Roderick claimed there were no mitigating circumstances for the killings and that he would be
blamed for the crime. He allegedly told them that if he
was arrested he planned to commit suicide as he could not
bear being jailed for twenty-five years. If he had been a
Catholic, Roderick said he would be seeking absolution,
but in a reply to a question (on the tape) from his uncle,
as to whether he would be looking forward to seeing his
parents on the other side, he replied, 'No.'

'These matters relate to the clearest confession to being
involved in murder a person could make without saying
"Yes, I did it,"' De Silva asserted. He went on to tell the
court that when Newall spoke to Elena Pedo he had 'tears
running down his face'. He shook her shoulder and the
words came tumbling out: 'I am a murderer. I am a murderer.' He told her he was responsible for the murder of
his parents. De Silva submitted that what emerged from
evidence was a carefully planned and brutally executed
double murder. It would seem that this was the first time
planning had been referred to in court. A *crime passionnel*
committed in the heat of an emotional moment is far more
understandable than the much more calculated process of
strategy. Could Roderick have been so steeped in hatred
for his parents that this was a possibility?

Roderick Newall's final legal attempts to stop the proceedings had failed earlier in the day when the colony's
Chief Justice, Alistair Kneller, rejected the application for
a judicial review. Chris Finch wanted the Supreme Court
to look at the legality of his arrest and transfer to Gibraltar,
but Chief Justice Kneller rejected the application as 'hope-
less in law'. The Crown was also successful in an application for costs by de Silva, despite Finch asking for an
adjournment to prepare for an application for legal aid.
The Crown rejected the assertion that Roderick was 'a

poor orphan who had squandered his patrimony'. Finch objected to the comment, describing it as unnecessary.

Later, the court was told how police dog handlers had found the lenses of glasses belonging to Nicholas Newall in the debris of the fire near the old family home, the Crow's Nest, at Greve de Lecq, seven months after the killings.

More evidence was presented by the Crown during the extradition proceedings in the afternoon. Referring to the dinner at the Sea Crest Hotel, de Silva said, 'That is the last the world was to see of Mr and Mrs Newall.' He contended that what had happened on the previous night of 9th October was highly significant in that Roderick Newall had flown over to the island and had stayed at his brother's house, La Falaise. Roderick had told police that he believed he had personally booked the table at the Sea Crest. De Silva then referred to the fact that Nicholas Newall hired the van in his own name. It was, he said, the Crown's suggestion that he was tricked into doing so and in fact was unwittingly hiring his own hearse. De Silva went on to allege that after the dinner at the Sea Crest the family returned home. 'The Crown case is that they were done to their death in their own home.' The only clothes that were never found were those Nicholas and Elizabeth had worn to the restaurant which indicated that they 'went to their final resting place before they went to bed.' De Silva went on to claim that this was what Roderick meant when he told his uncle and aunt in the secret tape recording, 'It pins it down to the night.'

De Silva argued that if the couple in fact died that night then Roderick in his statement to the police on 20th October 1987 set up a false alibi for himself. Newall told the police that he had left his parents 'preparing to go to bed and returned to his brother's home – La Falaise –'

166

where he slept until approximately 8 a.m., when he returned to his parents' home in his brother's car. They lunched together at 1 p.m., he stated, and he left at 3 p.m. De Silva pointed out that it was the Crown's contention that this was not the case. By dawn he suggested Roderick was still at the house, clearing up and disposing of items. De Silva had evidence from Sheila Cruickshank who lived next door to Mark Newall's house and whose windows overlooked the property. On 10th October she had noticed not only Mark Newall's white Toyota outside La Falaise but also the red van which the Crown say was the hired van.

Mrs Cruickshank was awoken just before 6 a.m. on Sunday 11th October. She heard doors slamming. She looked out of her hall window and saw the red van with its rear doors open and the white Toyota with its boot open. Although the lighting was dim she saw two men passing articles to each other.

If a jury were to come to the conclusion that one of those men was Roderick and this was a part of the process of disposal of incriminating articles, then it would follow that the story told to the police about lunching with his parents on the 11th October was a totally false account to hide the truth of having murdered his parents during the course of the previous night.

Mrs Maureen Bickerton lived opposite Mark Newall's house, La Falaise. She had noticed the white sports car outside the address previously. On 11th October at about 2 p.m. two young men who said they were from La Falaise came to her front door and wanted to know where they could burn rubbish. She saw them drive away in their red Falles hired van. If a jury comes to the conclusion that one of those men was Roderick Newall then again it means that the story he told of lunching with his parents is false.

All these glimpses of the evidence the police had amassed must have been deeply alarming for Roderick, but presumably, without the tape, they would have been only circumstantial. He must have realised that his confession to his uncle had condemned him and all he had been doing over the long months in Gibraltar had been debating technicalities. But the thought of the inevitable prison sentence was still horrifying him; his period on remand must have been a serious warning of what the future had in store for him.

On 11th October 1993, the extradition proceedings were adjourned when Pizzarello heard that the prosecution and defence wanted time to 'mutually edit some parts of statements to be read in open court'. Chris Finch also wanted the magistrate to consider an application for legal aid when the court resumed.

De Silva pointed out that J-cloth fragments found at the bonfire site near the Crow's Nest matched fragments found at the Newall home. These fragments, found on the hearth and just inside the door of the master bedroom, must indicate a major clean-up operation. De Silva continued that in Miami, Roderick took Crown witness Elena Pedo to see *Cape Fear*. Miss Pedo did not like it but Roderick said that 'it was good to live in fear'. Miss Pedo asked him if he was not afraid of going back to Britain to see the family, said de Silva. Roderick replied that he 'was only afraid of seeing his father's identical twin and not being able to keep his silence'. The Crown contended that in July 1992 Roderick had dinner with his aunt, Nancy Clarke. The conversation took a strange turn as they discussed mediums. Mrs Clarke said that she had been sent a message from his mother. Roderick then asked if she had seen her herself and Nancy Clarke replied that she had – on the night she had died. Roderick had then asked if his mother had said anything, and his aunt replied with the words, 'I told you he meant it. I told you it would happen but let the matter rest.' The Crown went on to state that Aunt Nancy had asked Roderick what had happened and he had replied, 'You would not understand.'

On the following day, Tuesday, 12th October, the *Jersey Evening Post* reported that Mark Newall had suffered facial cuts and bruises in an incident with another prisoner at La Moye prison the previous Sunday morning. The prison governor, Keith Wheeler, confirmed that the incident had taken place but had no connection with the fact that Mark Newall had failed to attend court when a further twenty-eight-day custodial remand was agreed.

In Gibraltar there was a further adjournment because Chris Finch had slipped over outside his office and broken his leg. It was rather as if the fates were intervening to keep Roderick permanently in Gibraltar. Would Pizzarello be struck down next? Or de Silva?

But when the hearing reopened, Roderick Newall gave up his fight against extradition. Perhaps the inside of the Moorish Castle prison was beginning to oppress him as much as the thought of La Moye. He also knew it was unlikely the fates would intervene again and impossible that he would soon be at the helm of the *Austral Soma*, sailing back to his wilderness. He would never be able to 'do the Ronnie Biggs'. It would be many years before he could even hope to be at sea again and Roderick knew that he might as well start serving them as quickly as possible.

He agreed to be brought back to stand trial with his brother Mark, who was still pleading not guilty to the murder charge. Finch accepted uncontested extradition on Wednesday, 20th October 1993, and Pizzarello told

Newall, 'I shall be committing you now to be taken out to Jersey.' He went on to say that Roderick had fifteen days in which to apply to Gibraltar's Supreme Court against the ruling, but Chris Finch replied that there would be no submission and the defence would be reserved for the hearing in Jersey. Roderick said nothing. As he left the court, surrounded by armed police – the Gibraltar authorities were still alarmed by the mysterious threat to spring him from the Moorish prison – the 'ex-army officer' who had used 'anti-surveillance techniques' and was generally considered highly dangerous, must have been in sombre mood. The La Moye prison loomed and the memories of his brief encounter with its walls sharpened. Last time his sentence had been a month. Next time it could be twenty-five years. Would he be able to bear it? On many of his court appearances Roderick carried a book, and on this occasion as he walked away with his armed escort it was seen that he had been reading *The Brethren* by Bob Woodward. Perhaps reading was one of the few mental activities that would offer temporary insulation from not just his crime but the thought of his sentence. When asked questions by the avid press hacks, he had no comment. A tinge of his former bravado was still with him but the defiant aura of escaping lone sailor had been reduced to one of grim foreboding.

Gittings said later in court, 'The feeling in Gibraltar is relief. Our only regret is that it has taken so long to reach the extradition.' But his words were a little over-dramatic; no one in Gibraltar, except for the hacks, really cared a damn for the locked-up Englishman.

On Friday, 5th November, the Governor of Gibraltar signed the warrant for Roderick's extradition and, at 7.25 a.m. on 6th November 1993, he was taken to Gibraltar airport and handed over to Detective Inspector Martin Fitzgerald who produced the warrant. He cautioned

Roderick and asked him if he understood its implications. He replied that he did. 'Is there anything that you want to know before you leave?' the Inspector asked, and Roderick replied, 'No, thank you.'

As they flew towards Jersey in a private plane, he was accompanied by his counsel, Advocate David Le Quesne. About seventy-five minutes into the flight Le Quesne handed Assistant Chief Officer Paul Marks a map of Jersey indicating the location of Nicholas and Elizabeth's grave on Greve de Lecq hill.

Marks then passed Le Quesne a larger scale map on which Roderick indicated two spots in Fields 389 and 390, giving a more precise location of where the bodies were. Later that day in Jersey he was formally charged with the murder of his parents and at 2.30 p.m. Detective Inspector Fitzgerald accompanied Roderick to the area in Greve de Lecq indicated by him earlier – which was only some 400 yards from the Crow's Nest. However, it soon became apparent that the landscape had changed dramatically since 1987 due to the hurricane and Roderick, handcuffed to a police officer, was unable to exactly pin-point the grave. Marks was concerned, convinced that Roderick was 'actually enjoying what he was doing. My own distinct impression was that he was giving us a bit of a run around and I actually spoke to the lawyer about that.' Marks wondered if Roderick was keeping them waiting, unable to bring himself to identify the exact location.

'He knew exactly where those graves were in my opinion. He just didn't want to say . . . the agenda was to buy a bit of time. I actually said to him, quietly, after dark . . . that the military instructor would not have been too impressed with this sort of thing. You should be able to take me straight to the spot.'

After seventy-five minutes he was returned to police

headquarters and the search continued. More officers were drafted in, and a team from Cornwall and Devon who had experience of this kind of project were flown over to assist.

The police also appealed to any members of the public who could remember how the site had appeared six years before, asking them to come forward as landscaping and a pond had considerably altered the layout of the area. Was the greatest irony about to take place? Were the corpses of Nicholas and Elizabeth Newall to remain obstinately lost for ever?

On Monday, 8th November, however, after Roderick had spent a further two hours at the site, he told the police how he had driven down the Greve de Lecq hill in the Falles hire van, realised he had overshot the site, reversed back up the hill, and eventually buried the bodies with his brother's help.

The search then concentrated on a corner of Field 391, but Roderick had already been taken back to La Moye prison before a mini excavator, already used in the search, removed soil to reveal black polythene lying in a shallow trench. When the polythene was examined a shoe and foot of Nicholas Newall was revealed. His body was wrapped in a green tarpaulin and the remains of Elizabeth Newall were found wrapped in a blue one. Their discovery, however predictable, shocked even the most ardent gossips on the island. Red refuse sacks were also found covering the corpses.

As the ambulance came and the bodies were removed, the police took off their helmets in respect.

The bodies of Nicholas and Elizabeth Newall were examined after the dig had been supervised by Home Office pathologist Dr Gyan Fernando. Eventually the corpses were taken from the unmarked graves where they had rested so long and transferred to the mortuary of the General Hospital in readiness for the post-mortem.

Dr Fernando carried out the examinations throughout the 11th and 12th of November. Once he had washed his face, Fernando instantly recognised Nicholas Newall. The bodies were well preserved and he found that both Nicholas and Elizabeth Newall died because of severe injuries to their heads. Many of these injuries were consistent with being struck by a blunt weapon which could have been a set of rice flails. But the more serious injuries done to the back of Nicholas's head were found to have been caused by a relatively sharp edged weapon. A laceration measured 8 cm. which was consistent with one of the edges of the pick axe that had been amongst the other equipment bought from Normans.

During the course of the post-mortem examinations, Dr Fernando removed the livers and stomach contents for examination by a toxicologist. Dr Alexander Allan, a forensic scientist at Aldermaston Laboratory, discovered the presence of phenobarbitone in the stomach contents and liver of Nicholas Newall. Phenobarbitone is used in the treatment of epilepsy and neither Nicholas nor Elizabeth suffered from the complaint. The side effects of the drug are similar to other barbiturates in that they induce drowsiness and sedation. When taken with alcohol there are dangers of overdosing and the risk of death is high.

Roderick's return to Jersey had already been widely reported. The *Evening Standard* had banner headlines:

I MURDERED PARENTS AFTER CHAMPAGNE PARTY, SAYS NEWALL
Former Army officer Roderick Newall today admitted killing his wealthy parents with his brother Mark.

Newall, 28, stood stony-faced before magistrates in St Helier as a guilty plea on the double murder charge was entered on his behalf.

Lloyds underwriter Nicholas Newall, 56, and his wife Elizabeth, 47, were bludgeoned to death in their luxury Jersey home after a champagne birthday party with their sons six years ago.

Their bodies have never been discovered but within hours of Newall's arrival on the island after extradition from Gibraltar he led police to woodlands where a search has been under way for three days.

At the ninety-second hearing in the Jersey police court Roderick, dressed as ever in blue blazer and jeans, was formally charged with the double murder 'on or about 10th October 1987'. His advocate, David Le Quesne, said, 'I'm instructed to plead guilty to both charges on behalf of my client.'

Magistrate David Trott then remanded Roderick in custody until 6th December and he was returned to La Moye prison handcuffed to two plain-clothes police officers.

Maureen Ellam was dubbed Miss Marple by the press, and the *Evening Standard* continued, 'The crime would have gone undetected had Newall not broken down and confessed when looking into the face of his father's identical twin.'

On Monday, 7th February 1994, Roderick Newall was re-interviewed by police officers. He denied purchasing the tarpaulins, the red refuse sacks and all the other items bought at the builders merchants the day before the murder. He also denied that the murders were premeditated and he denied that he used phenobarbitone dissolved in whisky to drug his father before killing him. He agreed that an iron bar found near the remains of the fire discovered at Greve de Lecq could have been part of a set of home made rice flails that he owned and which might have been used to kill his parents, but he was not specific about it.

At a committal hearing on Friday, 18th March 1994, Dr Fernando gave a full account of his findings. He told the court he had carried out autopsies on the exhumed bodies of Nicholas and Elizabeth on 11th and 12th November the previous year and had discovered a number of lacerations measuring from 1.5 cm. to 8 cm. long.

'In the case of the female skull there were a series of lacerations, seven individual lacerations, which ranged in length from 5.5 cm. to 1.5 cm.,' he said.

'In the case of the male skull two of the lacerations were at the front part of the head and six were found at the back of the head.

'The lacerations ranged in length from 8 centimetres to 3 centimetres.'

In both cases, Dr Fernando stated, although there were extensive fractures to the skull there were no other injuries to the bodies.

Crown Advocate Cyril Whelan, who took over from St Brelade Centenier Geoffrey Cornwall, and who had read the charges out in court, asked Fernando, 'Is it your opinion that the injuries were caused by blows to the head from some other person?'

'Yes,' the pathologist replied.

'What do you give as the cause of death?'

'In both cases the cause of death was multiple injuries to the head.'

Dr Fernando also confirmed that he was present at the Greve de Lecq field when the bodies were found. 'The mechanical digger unearthed what looked like a shoe in a black plastic liner. There were two human bodies and these were eventually exhumed without disturbing them. The bodies were fully dressed with all clothes and personal effects.' He added that the bodies had been found wrapped in large sheets of tarpaulin.

Odontologist David Lewin, a forensic science expert in analysing teeth and bite-marks, said that he was certain that the exhumed bodies were those of Nicholas and Elizabeth Newall. He compared radiographs and X-rays of Mr and Mrs Newall's dentistry records before they went missing with the jawbones of the bodies found.

Lewin continued, 'The findings were so unique, so much data there, that I am satisfied that the remains are those of the people I described.' He went on to tell the court that there was a standard procedure throughout the world of using dental records to identify human remains. 'In the case of the female body, I found that the number of teeth was the same and the body had seven filled teeth. I also found two wires in the jaw where surgery had been performed, which was a dramatic find. There was also one wisdom tooth which had not erupted in life – it was very distinct.'

Lewin added that, once again, the number of teeth in the male skull tallied with Mr Newall's dentistry records. 'Twenty teeth had fillings. Twenty is a very high number.'

During the months before the committal hearing, murder charges against Mark Newall were withdrawn and the island's magistrates heard him instead admit to helping his elder brother Roderick dispose of the bodies and evade justice.

At the hearing on 18th March, the press teams were in the police court to hear Roderick Newall confess to clubbing his parents to death with a rice flail. Outside TV camera crews from both the BBC and ITN joined Jersey's media behind the barriers as they waited for the prison van to approach. The Newall brothers eventually arrived between 10.30 and 10.45 a.m. for the case to be heard at 11 a.m.

Former Deputy and diplomat Sir Martin Le Quesne sat in the front row of the court listening to his son, Advocate David Le Quesne, represent Roderick and Mark Newall, who arrived in the court room at 11.15 a.m., both dressed in double-breasted suits, standing side by side in the dock, surrounded by detectives. Roderick was expressionless but Mark seemed drawn, his suit too big for his frame. They didn't look at each other as they listened to the charges read out by St Brelade Centenier Geoffrey Cornwall and to Crown Advocate Cyril Whelan as he introduced the case. There were only four witnesses – David Lewin, Dr Fernando, Martin Fitzgerald and Geoffrey Cornwall.

Strangely, there was laughter in court when UK odontologist David Lewin gave a résumé of his work history and experience which took a couple of minutes and was particularly extensive.

After he had finished, Assistant Magistrate David Trott turned to Advocate Whelan, saying, 'I think he has answered that question.'

'Brief laughter echoed around the court', as the *Jersey Evening Post* put it, but the atmosphere became tense as Detective Inspector Martin Fitzgerald read out Roderick's statement. He spoke quickly, stumbling over a sentence. He then read out Mark's. Both brothers said they were sorry for what they had done.

Advocate Whelan then stated, 'Under the circumstances, I have no difficulty in submitting that a prima facie case is established in relation to both accused, and that it is appropriate to seek an order that the case can be remanded to the Royal Court after the signing of the transcripts.'

The detectives then led the brothers back to the cells. The proceedings had lasted forty-five minutes and they had stared straight ahead throughout. There were no options left.

David Ellam told Philip Falle, 'My view is that when it suited me to use you I did so, to keep this thing going, to keep it in the public eye, to keep it uppermost in people's minds, and you quite willingly played along with me. But at the end of the day I feel that I am morally obliged to . . . talk openly about some of the things you and I have only been able to talk of privately.'

Maureen reflected on the unmarked graves. She claimed, like Nancy, to have dreamt of the dead Newall parents, but she apparently saw only Nicholas. 'It's a lovely place, it's nice, comfortable, it's easy, beautiful – a lovely place. I said that to Elizabeth's mother on the day they found them . . . All I could say was that it was a beautiful place. I think she understood about the peace and tranquillity. I think that she, like me, always felt that there was a minute chance that we'd all made a terrible mistake.'

She stated that when Nicholas Newall appeared in her vision, he was standing on the balcony outside her bedroom, pointing to the place where he and Elizabeth were buried. Maureen Ellam continued, 'I knew they were missing then and everyone was telling us that they were buried at sea, but the sea always gives up its dead, or parts of it. I didn't think they were in the water, my vision told me otherwise.'

In reply to a question about making contact with Roderick or Mark she said, 'No. I won't. If they want me . . .' and her voice trailed off to a whisper. 'What can I possibly want of them? It's over, it's done, but I don't see throwing good lives after bad achieves much either. Anyway, you can't bring them back.'

The only remaining question is whether Roderick Newall murdered his parents in drunken, spontaneous temper or as the result of a pre-arranged strategy. It is the case for the Crown that the equipment from Normans, the pheno-barbitone, the deep lacerations on his father's head, the convenient van hire, the money, the rooted hatred – all lurk in the background, waiting to be exposed.

When his parents were alive, Roderick had almost certainly lived with an increasing hatred, mainly directed at his father who had been so inflexibly dominating. Yet Nicholas and Roderick had a link – they both had a vision of what they wanted to do with their lives and went to considerable lengths to achieve their goals. Nicholas sailed to a tax haven and Roderick to the Falklands and the dream of becoming a rugged son of the sea. The only problem was that the father tried to block the son's freedom. Had Nicholas ever been thwarted? Perhaps he had at some stage, and maybe he was 'passing it on' as many parents have.

The American psychologist Baumrind sees authoritarian parents tending to demand very high standards of performance and behaviour from their offspring which require them to live up to standards already set by their own mother and father.

She says, 'Authoritarian parents do not encourage initiative or independence nor do they listen to their children's viewpoint or take notice of their ideas or preferences. They express little warmth; there are few hugs and cuddles or verbal expressions of affection ... They [the children] seem to have little sense of being able to control their environment and develop few strategies for doing so. These characteristics persist into adolescence, especially for boys.'*

In the end, Roderick may have had only one strategy – to wipe his parents out.

We all have hostile feelings towards our parents at some stage of our lives, and some of us may well fiercely hate them over a period of time and feel that we would like them to die – may even harbour thoughts of murder. But the vast majority do no such thing, never approaching that thin red line of divide between fantasy and intent. Roderick Newall's latent anger may well have simmered since his arid childhood and he could have seen his father as an obstacle to the future he so much desired – the future that was free of institutions, the great escape that he did attain in some small measure, except that he took his terrible secret and increasing guilt along with him. This was the albatross that hung round his neck, gradually sapping all his resolution so that in the end he was drawn back, away from his wilderness, eventually to concede defeat and take the police to the graves himself.

Mark Newall's loyalty to his brother throughout the entire process was total, and although he has admitted his culpability in helping to bury the bodies and mislead the police for so long, his love was all-embracing. Roderick is a tragic figure, a man of considerable talent whose slaughter of his parents was a deeply shocking event. But if only his father had showed him as much genuine love as his brother had, Nicholas Newall would surely have been alive today.

* A *Textbook of Psychology*, edited by John Radford and Ernest Govier, Routledge, 1991.

EPILOGUE

On Monday, 8th August 1994, the Royal Court in St Helier was packed with members of the police and local and national media as the sentencing of the Newall brothers was awaited. At two minutes before 10 am, the Bailiff of Jersey, Sir Peter Crill, arrived and the nine red-robed jurats took their seats. (Jurats are the local dignitaries of Jersey who are able to assess cases and determine sentences.)

Seconds after the prayers had been read Roderick and Mark Newall were led into the court, flanked by police officers. Both wore the same grey suits they had worn at their police committal. Roderick wore a tie with a navy emblem and Mark's was patterned. The brothers had their hands clasped in front of them and were staring straight ahead.

As the charges were read out Roderick, looking pale, cast his eyes down and slowly bowed his head. Mark, too, cast down his eyes, swallowed and briefly clenched his teeth. The Newall brothers' freedom was over; their much delayed sentence about to be given.

Roderick and Mark then took their seats behind their Advocate, David Le Quesne, and listened as the Attorney

General, Michael Birt, put forward his submission for the prosecution, reading from a forty-eight page document. Roderick sat listening intently, Mark looked down, twisting his thumbs as they were handed copies of the Attorney General's address. Gradually the details of the case unfolded yet again. The current officers involved in the case, DI Martin Fitzgerald, Sergeant Charles MacDowall, DC Charles Cadnam and Assistant Chief Officer Paul Marks were in court to listen as were those who had retired, such as Graham Nimmo.

All the details in the submission have already been addressed in this book, but there are some that are worth repeating in the light of the degree of premeditation that may have been present in the carrying out of the murders.

Michael Birt stated that: 'The court will appreciate that the evidence suggested that Roderick was not telling the whole truth in his voluntary statement where he refers to killing both his parents with a set of rice flails which he found in the house. Accordingly, the police interviewed him again on 7 February 1994. In that interview Roderick maintained that he used just one weapon which was a set of rice flails, but was unable to give any assistance as to what they looked like as there were, he said, so many different types of rice flails. He thought that some did have sharp leading edges and that some were made of metal. He was then shown the piece of metal referred to previously which was found in the fire. He said that he thought there was a set of rice flails which were like that and that that might have been the weapon which he used.

'Following this interview, evidence was obtained from a Mr Julian Mead, an expert in martial arts. He confirmed that rice flails, or nunchakus, as they are more correctly known, consist of two bits of wood – or occasionally metal in case of home-made rice flails – of just over a foot in length, of a diameter of about one and a quarter inches at the narrow end and two inches at the wide end, joined by a chain about 8 inches in length. They are either circular, octagonal, or, very occasionally, square in shape. Mr Mead gave it as his opinion that there were no nunchakus that had any sharp edges that would cause the type of injury that would be inflicted by the cutting edge of a mattock. The pathologist, Dr Fernando, has confirmed in a further statement that even the sharpest of rice flails, namely one with a square shape and therefore an edge with an angle of 90 degrees, could not have caused the injuries to the back of Nicholas Newall's head.

'The Crown says that Roderick is not telling the truth in this respect, as his version of events is inconsistent with the forensic pathological evidence which refers to two very different sorts of weapon having been used, one of which, namely the heavy weapon with a cutting edge, could not have been rice flails as alleged by Roderick.

'In his statement, Roderick also suggests that the murders arose on the spur of the moment. The Crown says that there is some circumstantial evidence to suggest that this was not so.'

At this point, Mr Birt began a detailed submission relating to the purchase of items from Norman Ltd on 10 October 1987.

'There is another aspect of the evidence which lends support to the contention that Roderick is not telling the whole truth in his statement.

'I have previously referred to the occasion on which Roderick pointed to a whisky bottle and said to [Elena] Pedo, his Brazilian girlfriend: "That was responsible for what happened." It may be said that this lends support to what Roderick is now saying in his voluntary statement, namely that the murders happened in anger on the spur of the moment following a night when he had clearly been drinking. Yet in his talk with his uncle, Stephen Newall, part of the conversation went as follows:

'Stephen Newall: "What about some mitigating circumstances, you know, like a crazy drunken rage or something? Does that mitigate your internal thing as well?"

'Roderick: "No."

'Stephen: "Well, if you . . ."

'Roderick: "That wasn't involved. I mean from the point of view of going to court, then yes, one could – (*telephone rings*)."

'Roderick is now indeed "going to court". Is he now doing what he there previewed, namely suggesting that the killings occurred in a "crazy drunken rage or something" when the truth was, as he indicated to Stephen, different?

'For these reasons, the Crown is unable to accept that Roderick has been truthful in his statement. He has lied consistently throughout this investigation, and the Crown says that, even now, he cannot bring himself to face the whole truth, namely that, at some time before 11.11 am on Saturday 10 October, he decided to murder both his father and his mother.'

The defence was later to challenge these statements.

Later, Birt's submission stated, 'He (Roderick) has pleaded guilty to murdering both his parents by bludgeoning them to death in their own home. He has offered no explanation of his actions save to say that a heated argument developed "in which many old wounds were re-opened". The Crown says that there is strong evidence to suggest that the murders did not occur on the spur of the moment as he suggests. Whether they did or not, he struck his father repeatedly on the head while he was lying stunned or unconscious on the ground. He used a heavy weapon with a cutting edge. It was a scene of considerable violence. He also struck his mother repeatedly on the head with sufficient force to kill her when she too must have been lying on the ground. For this he used a different weapon. It was a terrible crime. There is only one sentence which the law provides in cases of murder, and accordingly I move that concurrent sentences of life imprisonment be passed upon Roderick Newall on the two counts of the indictment against him.

'I have considered whether to invite the court to make a recommendation for a minimum period of imprisonment, as it is empowered to do by virtue of Article 1(2) of the Homicide (Jersey) Law, 1986. It is my understanding that, in England, where they have a similar provision, such recommendations tend to be reserved for those cases where, from the nature of the facts of the case, the accused appears to represent a danger to the public at large.

'Although this was a double murder, it lies within a domestic context, and accordingly I do not invite the court to make a recommendation.'

Birt then turned to the case of Mark Newall.

'He is aged 27, having been born on 22 June 1966. He has no previous convictions other than a minor driving conviction. He has admitted the offence of assisting his brother after the commission of the offence, and accordingly he is to be sentenced on the basis that he was not involved in any way until after the murders. Mark's involvement can be summarised by the following actions which he took to assist his brother escape justice:

'1. He helped him wrap up the bodies in the tarpaulins, transport them in the dead of night to Greve de Lecq, carry them over 100 metres and then dig a grave to hide both bodies.

'2. He then returned with Roderick to the house and set about cleaning the house so as to remove all trace of the terrible crime which had taken place, including disposal of the weapon or weapons.

'3. He then made statements to the police on 20 and 21 October to support Roderick. But these statements were false. In the early hours of 11 October 1987, Mark and Roderick Newall had not returned together to La Falaise. They did not awake between 8 and 8.30. They did not have breakfast as described at 9 Clos de l'Atlantique. They did not find their parents asleep in bed. They did not leave the house and return to a cosy family Sunday morning, reading Sunday newspapers and sharing Sunday lunch. Mark's statement in support of Roderick's was an intricate and deliberate lie, woven to establish a consistent story so as to provide Roderick Newall with a false alibi for the time of the murders.

'4. In November 1987 Mark was again interviewed at length. He again lied and maintained his story, thereby providing Roderick with an alibi.

'5. In the autumn of 1990, together with Roderick, he applied for a declaration of death. He swore an affidavit in support which he knew was false. On 3 January 1991 he gave evidence on oath before the Royal Court when he again lied as to what had happened.

'6. Following the obtaining of the declaration of death by the Royal Court on 3 January 1991, he was interviewed at length by the police and maintained his false story.

'7. He looked after the family finances and sent money to Roderick as necessary. No doubt this may have been from the half-share of the estate that belonged to Roderick, but it enabled Roderick to remain overseas. It also enabled Roderick to delay the extradition proceedings in Gibraltar from August 1992 to October 1993.'

Mr Birt then quoted legal precedents on the level of sentencing.

'I take into account, by way of mitigation, his guilty plea and the background information referred to in the reports. Nevertheless, this was a serious offence on the part of Mark Newall which led to a murderer escaping justice for six years. Indeed, if Roderick had not confessed to his uncle, Mark's conduct might well have resulted in no one being brought to justice for the murder of Nicholas and Elizabeth Newall. In the circumstances I move for a sentence of six years concurrent on each count.'

Advocate David Le Quesne said that the defence firmly rejected the Crown's allegation that the murders were not a spontaneous crime, and he added that the evidence put forward by them was 'meagre and unreliable and certainly does not establish their allegations beyond reasonable doubt'. Le Quesne told the court:

'I propose to deal first with Roderick Newall, who has pleaded guilty to two charges of murder. The majority of my address will be directed towards rebutting the Crown's suggestion that the murders were not spontaneous, as Roderick Newall has stated and the evidence indicates, but were planned in advance.

'I then shall turn to Mark Newall. He is a separate defendant and must be treated as such: he has pleaded guilty to very different, less serious, non-violent offences. The penalty for him is not mandatory, and I shall plead mitigating facts which I hope will satisfy the court that it can safely and properly impose substantially lower sentences than those suggested by the Crown.

'The court has heard little from the Crown about the family background beyond the statement that the relationship between the boys and their parents was "cold and complex". On my clients' specific instructions it will hear little from me on this subject, but that gap is partially filled by careful background reports prepared for the court by the Probation Service. The court will have seen that the material in both probation reports concerning the family relationships is similar; this is not surprising and it indicates that the parents' treatment of their children was broadly consistent.

'In his statement made to the police on 6 November 1993, Roderick said:

'"Briefly, the circumstances were that after Mark left, my parents and I were alone in the house and continued talking and drinking in the sitting-room of their house. A heated argument developed in which many old wounds were reopened. It came to a head with my father and I standing face to face as I told him what I thought about him – things which I had never said before. He pushed me and I fell, hitting my head on the dining-room table. I fell beside a box of my possessions which I had earlier sorted and had removed from the attic. On top of this box was a pair of rice flails which I grabbed and used to club my father. I remember him falling. My next memory is of finding myself sitting on the floor of the hall. I got up, went into the sitting-room and saw my father's body. I could not find a pulse. In a complete panic I checked the kitchen and then the bedroom where I found my mother's body which triggered my memory of also attacking her with a flail and her falling."

'Roderick was there describing, six years after the event and in the rather formal language which so often is seen in statements made to the police, the killing by him of his parents after an argument suddenly and spontaneously developed into violence. You will recollect from what the Attorney General has said that Roderick Newall, his mother and father had, between the three of them, drunk two bottles of champagne at the restaurant and three bottles of wine with the meal and liqueurs after the meal;

when they returned home they started drinking whisky. A family argument between these three people, fuelled as they were with drink, was likely to lead to trouble. It took an assault from Nicholas Newall – he pushed Roderick Newall who fell and hit his head, to light that fuel.

'The Crown has said that it does not believe this scenario. It says that this was not a spontaneous crime, but that it was planned by Roderick Newall. This allegation is firmly rejected by the defence.

'The Crown bases its allegation of premeditation on two matters. First, the murder weapon: the Crown says that the injuries which caused the death of Nicholas Newall could not have been caused by rice flails and probably were caused by a mattock purchased for the purpose at Normans Ltd. Second, the Crown relies upon a shopping expedition which it says Roderick Newall made to Normans Ltd on the morning of Saturday 10 October 1987 in order to purchase certain items which were required for the killings which he planned for that night.'

At this point, Advocate Le Quesne gave his detailed rebuttal of the prosecution claims relating to the murder weapon and the purchase from Norman Ltd.

'I now turn to some general matters which tend to cast doubt upon the proposition that Roderick Newall planned the murders.

'Roderick Newall was a lieutenant in the army and had spent some time as an instructor. He had also worked as an instructor in an Outward Bound school. He was a physical, practical man who later sailed vast distances single-handed.

'He was trained in the army to plan and execute operations. The requirement for careful planning is drummed into every army officer.

'It is alleged that, for whatever motive (and no motive is suggested by the Crown), he planned to kill his parents. If it was a long-term plan, why did he not arrange an accident from the boat on one of his frequent sailing trips with them in the Mediterranean? Perhaps he only concocted the plan on the Saturday morning or within a day or two, but in that case why the urgency and still, why the lack of proper planning?

'(a) Why plan a murder in which he inevitably would be the prime suspect?

'(b) Why the highly public and visible dinner at the Seacrest restaurant?

'(c) Why plan a murder in such a way as to cause a blood-bath?'

'(d) What was he planning to do with the bodies? Did he really plan to drive at dead of night right across the island on a Saturday night? What if he had been stopped by the police?

'(e) Did he really plan to bury them in a place to which he would have to carry the bodies one hundred yards across a meadow from the road?

'(f) The Crown has referred to "the labour required efficiently to package two bodies, which must have been covered in blood, to lift them, to transport them, to pick a site for the grave in the middle of the night."

'This precisely accords with Roderick Newall's assertion that there was no premeditation; only after the killings was the problem of picking a site for a grave considered.

'(g) What if another car had passed along the road while the bodies were being dragged across the meadow?

'(h) Why plan to dig graves, which would have to be done by torchlight, in a place where the torches easily could be seen from the road?

'(i) Why no plan for disposing of the evidence? Why

have to ask a neighbour of Mark's, the next day, if bonfires were permitted at Noirmont Common?

'None of this gives the impression of planning, let alone planning by a young army officer. It rings true of a sudden, terrible, violent episode resulting from a frenzy fuelled by drink and provoked by his father pushing him over.

'Roderick Newall appears to have confessed twice to the killings, before formally confessing to the police. The Crown suggests that the words which he used to his uncle and aunt show that he even then was preparing to give a false excuse to the court for what he had done.

'The Gibraltar magistrate described the conversation in Scotland between Roderick Newall and his uncle and aunt as a "verbal ballet". Stephen Newall's question to which the Attorney General has referred must be read carefully in order to understand the answer:

'"What about some mitigating circumstances, you know, like a crazy drunken rage or something? Does that mitigate your internal thing as well?"

'Answer: "No. That wasn't involved. I mean, from the point of view of going to court, then yes, one could . . ."

'The context, and the particular question to which Roderick Newall was replying, referred to his "internal thing". In other words his inner turmoil; he was saying that it was not lessened by the circumstances, although it might be mitigation in court.

'By contrast with the staged confession with Stephen and Gaye Newall, Roderick Newall's first confession a year earlier was not invited or manipulated; it was totally spontaneous and made in circumstances which suggest he was talking from the heart. Roderick Newall was alone at home with his girlfriend, in Brazil . . . he started to weep and was comforted by her. He took her shoulders and shook them and repeated: "I'm a murderer: I'm a murderer." He then pointed to a bottle of whisky and said: "That was responsible for what happened." This confession bears the hallmarks of spontaneity and truth.

'I have been specifically instructed not to attempt to excuse Roderick Newall for his crimes by indulging in character assassination of the deceased. Roderick Newall accepts that his crimes are inexcusable. However, within the confines of my instructions, I think I can properly say firstly that such crimes do not occur in normal, happy families; and secondly that perhaps some insight into the background of this case may be gleaned from a remark not of Roderick Newall but of Stephen Newall, his uncle. I refer you to the family conversation in Scotland which, in the absence of any other evidence, provided the reason for the arrests in this case. Stephen Newall said: "We of course watched from the sidelines (and saw) two very badly treated little boys . . ."

'Its importance lies in the fact that, coming from a third party in a position to know the facts, it cannot be tainted by being thought self-serving by the court.

'Further insights into the family relationships, described by the Crown as "cold and complex", are contained in the probation report.

'As is apparent from the sentiments expressed in that family conversation and in what Roderick Newall said to his girlfriend in Brazil, the memories of the events of that night have haunted every day of Roderick Newall's life and will presumably continue so to do until he dies. Before summoning up the courage in Gibraltar to do as he has done, he made several serious attempts to commit suicide. He did summon up that courage to return, although his Gibraltar lawyer was advising him that he could win on appeal.

'An additional reason for the events of that night

troubling Roderick Newall lies in the presence beside him in court of his brother. Because he sought his brother's help, and received it, he has dragged his brother down with him and it is not just he but they who now suffer imprisonment.

'Roderick Newall is no danger to anyone else in society. The facts and pressures that led to these events are necessarily incapable of repetition. He has no history of violence. Indeed he had not only an unblemished character but also to his credit positive good service to his country as a soldier.

'In all the circumstances I invite you to pass the sentences you have to, but to leave the actual time to be served before he is rehabilitated into society to the relevant authorities who will guard and observe him.

'I now turn to Mark Newall, and again I am instructed not to speak ill of the dead. My client is content that the court should bear in mind two things said by Stephen Newall when talking to Roderick Newall in the hotel in Scotland. First, his reference to "two very badly treated little boys": second, his reference to Mark as the one who "always came in for the heavy end of the thing". The background report gives further material which will enable the court, using his wisdom and experience, to make the obvious inference. Suffice it to say that Mark Newall knew from an early age that his parents disliked him, and as he grew older, so he grew apart from them.

'Mark Newall left school and went straight into banking: he was determined to excel, probably in order to prove both to himself and his parents that he was a capable being and worthy of respect. He worked long hours and his application and ability were soon noticed, and he joined the fast stream. In 1987 he was a Eurobond broker at the age of 21; he was successful and well paid. A successful career lay ahead, and, as the probation report shows, that success was at the time of his arrest in Paris. He was independent of his parents, and it was they who now relied upon him, for they required his management of their finances: indeed his income already exceeded theirs.

'From the extracts of Roderick Newall's and Mark Newall's statements already read to the court, we know how Mark Newall became involved in the crime. In the small hours of the Sunday morning he was summoned by his brother who was on the point of suicide. One can imagine the scene which met his eyes when he arrived – his brother cradling a shotgun and threatening to kill himself: his father lying dead in the sitting-room surrounded by blood: his mother lying elsewhere in the house, dead, in a pool of blood. Mark Newall was aged 21 years.

'A snap decision had to be made by this young man: help his brother, or call the police. There was no halfway point, because if he did not help, his brother clearly was going to shoot himself. Once he had taken the wrong decision, which was to help, the tragedy was into its second act. There really was no turning back, for to have helped his brother that night, and told the police the next day, would have been treachery. Further, once he and his brother had applied their undoubted intelligence to covering the crime, Mark Newall was himself too involved to draw back.

'Thereafter, Mark Newall's life was on the edge of the abyss. He knew that he had committed a serious crime, and he knew that, at any moment, the storm might break.

'He knew that he and his brother were prime suspects, and he knew the anguish of his family – particularly his grandmother in Scotland with whom he kept in close contact ... yet he dared do nothing. The higher he rose in his career, the further he had to fall.

'The third act of the tragedy opened with Roderick Newall confessing to his uncle and aunt in Scotland. Seven months later, Mark Newall was arrested in Paris to await extradition for murder. It is to his credit that he did not contest the extradition. Indeed, he stated to the police officers when he was arrested that he was willing to return to Jersey immediately, and his counsel in Paris confirmed this to the judge. He was then held on murder charges until his brother's return.

'I ask the court to accept that, effectively, everything has flowed from the decision taken in 1987. It was not a decision which Mark Newall could review every few months. Once it was made, Mark Newall was set on a course from which it became increasingly difficult to deviate. As you read in the probation report, he tried to submerge himself in work and, at one stage, drink. Whether Mark Newall's decision would have been different had he been contemplating covering up the murders of two parents whom he loved and respected is a matter for speculation. The fact that there was no such love and respect in either direction makes his decision easier to understand.

'Mark Newall has lived under the sword of Damocles since 1987; he has not just had to live with the threat [to] his freedom, but also with the knowledge that many, including his family, had labelled him as a murderer.

'For 17 months he has been in custody, and for much of that time – until his brother returned to Jersey – he was charged as a murderer. He knows he faces a further term of imprisonment.

'Mark Newall has lost his job, his position in the world, and his friends.

'All of this is the result of a wrong decision made under the threat of his brother blowing his brains out, when aged 21.

'This is not a crime for personal gain. This is not a crime of violence.

'Mark Newall poses no conceivable threat to the public, and the facts are such that there is no likelihood of him repeating the crime.

'Mark Newall is of good character, having only one minor driving offence against his name. Mark Newall must be given full credit for not contesting his extradition and for pleading guilty immediately the correct charges were presented to him. This is not a case where a defendant has no realistic option to pleading guilty, and therefore receives reduced credit. Without Mark Newall's plea and confession, the Crown effectively had no admissible evidence against him.

'This is such an unusual case that the court need not be concerned with setting an example or sending a signal. The court is left, therefore, with the task of punishing Mark Newall so as to mark its disapproval of his conduct. My plea to the court on behalf of Mark Newall is that it should look at the extraordinary facts of this case: both the family circumstances and the personal pressure this young man was under. The court can be merciful and just. It would be right, in my submission, to start consideration of sentence at a lower point than that suggested by the Crown. It would also be right to give the fullest possible credit for the guilty plea – which can be up to one-third the sentence which otherwise would be imposed. I submit that the court may then review the mitigating factors, and may, in its mercy, further reduce the sentence.'

Roderick Newall was given a double life sentence for the murder of his parents and the Bailiff, Sir Peter Crill, told him, 'Throughout the ages, the crimes of patricide and matricide have attracted particular odium. The court shares that view. But the court notes that you have accepted that your crimes are inexcusable, and so they are.'

He then told Mark Newall that he was to be sentenced to six years in prison, despite the fact that a minority of the jurats who determined his sentence had wanted to impose a higher term on him.

Both Roderick and Mark Newall were led away without betraying emotion – a trait that the family specialised in but the brothers had had so much need of.

There are two final episodes to relate: Nancy Clarke is concerned about the way the case was handled by the Jersey authorities. The Attorney General ruled that only evidence directly applicable to Roderick Newall's confession was admissible and she is certain that much remains to be told. She is also forgiving and told the *Telegraph*, 'Elizabeth would have expected me to look after them no matter what had happened. They are still her sons. Although I have pressed for them to be punished, once they have served their time they will still be relatively young men and we will have to solve the problem of how we're all going to settle down together. That is what being a family is all about.'

Mark Newall, however, is not so forgiving and has made it clear that he will fight to keep the hundreds of thousands of pounds he inherited. He stated that his aunt and uncle were 'greedy and distasteful' for trying to deprive him and Roderick of their wealth – despite the fact that while awaiting sentence, Roderick had issued a statement saying that he wanted nothing to do with his inheritance. David Le Quesne said that there was no statute in Jersey, as in England, which prevents a person benefiting from the proceeds of a crime. He understood that the claim against Roderick would be under common law, on the same grounds. Le Quesne added, 'But I am puzzled about the grounds of a claim against Mark. Mark had no part in the murder. His involvement began after his parents were dead. I do not see how you can be prevented from profiting from somebody else's crime.' Even if the Newall relatives' law suit is successful, however, the court may not be able to allocate them much more than the value of the Jersey bungalow.

Mark Newall could well retain his fortune while his more impetuous brother spends many years in jail. As Nancy Clarke believes, there is much to be told about the Newall brothers' story in the past – and, no doubt, in the future.

APPENDIX

The Argument over Premeditation

The argument in court between the prosecution and defence centred on the question of premeditation – and a series of purchases made at builders merchants Norman Ltd at 11.11 on Saturday 10 October 1987, just hours before the murders.

Attorney-General Mr Michael Birt maintained that equipment including one of the alleged murder weapons, as well as spades and tarpaulins of the kind used to wrap the bodies was bought there by Roderick Newall, who must therefore have planned murder.

Advocate David Le Quesne claimed that the victims were killed with a set of martial arts rice flails, picked up by Roderick Newall after he had been pushed to the floor by his father in a drunken argument, and that the crime was committed in the heat of the moment. The tarpaulins used in the disposal of the bodies belonged to the victims and were taken from their home, he said.

Items similar to those later found buried with Nicholas and Elizabeth Newall were included in the purchases made by a young, fair-haired man at the Commercial Buildings store at the time when Roderick was known to have been in the vicinity, Mr Birt told the court.

The Norman's purchase included a green Monarflex tarpaulin, a blue Multitarp tarpaulin measuring 15 feet by 18 feet, some red plastic rubble bags with ties and a mattock capable of inflicting a sharp wound eight centimetres long, said the Attorney-General, adding: 'Hours later, buried with the bodies were a green Monarflex tarpaulin, a blue tarpaulin cut from an original sheet approximately 15 feet by 18 feet and some red plastic bags with ties. One of the skulls had, among other injuries, a sharp fracture eight centimetres long.' The mattock bought at Norman's has never been found.

The identity of the purchaser was not recorded because he paid £103.42 in cash and Advocate Le Quesne said that, although Roderick was in the area – having been to South Pier Shipyard to look for a boat for his brother to buy for diving when he returned to live in the island – there was evidence to show that the man was not Roderick.

The goods were sold by shop assistant Tina Collins, who thought that she saw the person who had bought them in the shop again in July 1988. That man – young and fair-haired like Roderick – turned out to be Sigurdur Hafsteinsson, whose denial of having made the purchases was accepted, said Mr Birt. In a photographic identification, in which Roderick's picture was included with 11 others, Miss Collins stated that none of the pictures was that of the purchaser, but Mr Birt argued that it was not surprising that she could not identify a customer nine months after the event.

There was, however, considerable evidence to suggest that the purchaser was Roderick, he added, citing:

The evidence in the grave.

A lack of expert evidence to support Roderick's claim that the rice flail was the murder weapon.

Norman Ltd were the sole Jersey agent for Monarflex tarpaulins from 1984. Nicholas Newall's body was wrapped in tarpaulin which could have come from a bigger sheet and burnt green plastic found in a bonfire near the Newalls' old family home could have come from a Monarflex tarpaulin.

The blue tarpaulin in which Elizabeth Newall's body was wrapped was of the same chemical composition as the Multitarp one sold on 10 October 1987 and had been cut from a larger sheet, estimated at 15 feet by 17 feet. Blue plastic and an eyelet of the type used by Multitarp were found in the bonfire.

The only outlet in Jersey selling blue Multitarp in the relevant size was Norman Ltd. Only two were sold between their first stocking it and 10 October 1987. The first was traced and inspected by police; the second was the one sold that day to a 'young fair-haired man'.

No other blue tarpaulin of any make was sold in the relevant size by a Jersey outlet up to and including 10 October 1987, although there are incomplete records from three suppliers who have since gone out of business.

Only two outlets sold the red plastic rubble bags, one of which was found on Nicholas Newall's body.

Only Norman Ltd stocked all three items – green Monarflex tarpaulin, blue Multitarp tarpaulin and red plastic bags with ties – before 10 October 1987.

Nicholas Newall had two accounts at Norman's but had bought no tarpaulins, contradicting the defence claim that they were taken from the Newalls' home. The parents could not have been the cash purchasers on 10 October because they were having coffee with friends David and Maureen Ellam at the time.

David Ellam, who helped the Newalls with their DIY work, said that he had never noticed tarpaulins in their garage or house.

Dismissing the prosecution evidence concerning alleged premeditation and the Norman Ltd purchase as 'meagre and unreliable', Advocate Le Quesne said that the mattock claimed by the Crown to have been used had never been found and that Roderick was adamant that he used rice flails.

Of the three sets of wounds described by the pathologist – to the rear and front of Nicholas Newall's head and to Elizabeth Newall's head – the latter two were consistent with Roderick's claim and the former set, claimed Advocate Le Quesne, could have been caused by a sharp-ended rice flail.

Had the fatal injuries to the back of Nicholas's head, consisting of six lacerations accompanied by extensive fractures, been caused by a mattock, it would have meant Roderick leaving the room after hitting his father with the rice flails in order to fetch a mattock to finish him off. He would have hit Nicholas one full blow, leaving an eight-centimetre cut through the scalp, followed by five lesser blows delivered in such a way that the full face of the blade did not even come into contact with the head, said Advocate Le Quesne, who added: 'It seems a strangely tentative way to use the weapon if the intention was to kill.'

He also placed a different interpretation to that of the prosecution on evidence given by a martial arts expert, who said that the wounds were inconsistent with a rice flail, or nunchaku, used properly. The weapon was, indeed, not used properly because it was a 'sudden frenzied attack' and not premeditated, said the lawyer. He suggested that ten fatal wounds were caused by the sharp angle at the top of the rice flail, and that all the injuries were caused by the same weapon, used differently.

Turning to the Norman Ltd purchase, Advocate Le Quesne agreed that Roderick was in the Commercial Buildings area on 10 October 1987 but was not the man who bought the tarpaulins, spades and mattocks because:

Had he been, he would not have volunteered the information that he was in the area.

There was no evidence identifying him as the man, but there was evidence that he was not.

The man was described as stocky, with glasses and blond curly hair, aged 28 to 30 and accompanied by a female, none of which applied to Roderick, who was 22 at the time.

Roderick did not attempt to conceal his movements that day. If he had wanted to buy tarpaulins, he could have done so at the boatyard.

The green tarpaulin in which Nicholas's body was wrapped could have come from any of the 'innumerable' such tarpaulins sold by Norman Ltd before the day in question, or have been bought by Mr Newall from another supplier in Jersey before 1984, or on one of his many trips to the UK.

The Crown had not even established that the blue material in which Elizabeth's body was found was from a Multitarp tarpaulin, and had produced no evidence about the age of the tarpaulins.

The Ellams were not great friends of the Newalls. Between their meeting and the murders, the Newalls were in Jersey for only four months. It was 'preposterous' to suggest that, at that stage in his life, Nicholas Newall suddenly needed advice on tools and equipment from a new acquaintance. There was therefore no evidence that he did not keep tarpaulins in his garage.

The three red rubble sacks in the grave could have come from at least two other outlets. If six were bought from Norman Ltd for a premeditated murder, where were the other three?

There were other types of plastic sacks in the grave, suggesting a 'desperate search at the house for anything that could be used'.

Despite intensive searches, there was no trace of other items bought at Norman's, including a mattock, torches and batteries, sisal rope, upholstery cleaner, a saw and spades.

The upholstery cleaner bought at Norman's was of a different make to that used by the Newalls' cleaner, but the one in the grave was not.

The bodies were bound with black nylon twine found at the house, not the sisal.

The house, shed and garage at Clos de l'Atlantique were full of equipment that could be used in the disposal of bodies and there would have been no need to go to Norman's. That and the fact that items not from Norman's were used meant that Roderick could not have been the mystery purchaser.